POWERFUL
NETWORKING

POWERFUL
NETWORKING

JOHN LOCKETT

ORION BUSINESS
BOOKS

First published in Great Britain in 1999 by
Orion Business
An imprint of The Orion Publishing Group Ltd
Orion House, 5 Upper St Martin's Lane,
London WC2H 9EA

A CIP catalogue record for this book
is available from the British Library.

ISBN 0–75282–080–X

Typeset by Deltatype Ltd, Birkenhead
Printed and bound in Great Britain
by Clays Ltd, St Ives plc.

CONTENTS

INTRODUCTION – WHY NETWORK?

Networking has become one of the key words underpinning the new way of working – one of the most critical of the new skills that we are all encouraged to learn at work. Despite this, and although many management texts include an entry or two, it has rarely been the core subject of a whole book. We are being told that we should be doing more of it, and yet no one is telling us how or why.

The aim of this book is to address the how, why and who of networking to enable you to grasp the key skills in a relatively short time so that you can do some serious networking yourself. The skills you will learn can be used both at work and in your social and recreational life – and that will help you in a number of ways. Before moving on to the positive development of the skills of networking, we'll review some of the negative approaches that people seem to have to the idea of networking and get them out of the way, so that you can spend the rest of the book focused on the positive benefits and learning the important skills.

WHY PEOPLE DON'T NETWORK

The word 'network' has developed some unfortunate constructs along the way – for some it reminds them of old school ties, company politics, gaining an inside track, blowing your own trumpet and generally schmoozing around at work rather than doing anything really productive. For many people it involves little more than handing out business cards at conferences and having the occasional power lunch. For others, it is a dark and frightening science, involving targeting key people and setting out to use them mercilessly to gain access to the hidden market of fat cat jobs and lucrative business contracts.

The perception that people have of networks depends largely on their own position in relation to a particular network. Insiders see it as a positive force and a productive and stimulating part of their lives. Outsiders see networks as the process which ensures that the privileged few get the gold and the people outside get the dross. There is no doubt that over the years, certain closed networks have led to a restriction in opportunities – mainly the middle-class male networks, emanating from membership of the same closed elite institutions, which had been a bar to the progress of non-members. The answer which many people have found to the closed, restrictive networks has been the development of new and exciting networks with open access and constantly changing membership.

The old boy networks of school ties and regimental honour had their place in a world where corporate loyalty and conformity were prized above anything else. They did, however, create organisations that were stiff and stodgy, lacking new ideas because of the stranglehold of a white, male, middle-class and middle-aged elite. In the new world of diversity and creativity, the idea of networking is a positive force, breaking down barriers and giving people access to new ideas and new contacts.

Yet still some people find networking difficult and painful. In my discussions with managers, a number of themes emerge in relation to networking and the barriers to doing it effectively. For many people, networking is embarrassing as they believe it involves blowing their own trumpet and indulging in self-promotion; they think that it should be enough that they do a competent job without having to go around telling people how good they are. This is a typical response to networking which prevents many people from developing a personal network – it is based on the mistaken view that networking is somehow devious and underhanded; that it involves politics and unfair influencing and that 'real work' is only about individual effort. Work is at the centre of networking – both literally and figuratively – and linking your efforts with those of other professionals is increasingly important for even the most reclusive specialist.

Others see networking as an additional hassle in an increasingly busy life. Everyone is so busy today that to spend time with other people is seen as a further unnecessary time stealer. Making appointments, writing thank you letters, keeping track of people's addresses and going to external meetings seems for many to take up valuable time that should be devoted to 'real work'. Networking is important for many reasons and if done effectively generates a good return for the use of time. Later in this chapter, I will examine six reasons for networking, all of which can lead to improvements in productivity and overall effectiveness.

Others shy away from networking because

they are contemptuous of the 'old boy net-work', having seen it working in an insidious way in their organisation. They prefer to gain preferment on merit, and rightly so – but they have to ask what 'merit' means in today's workplace. Organisations are increasingly big and complex, working in a world that is equally complicated – work now involves teamwork, cross functional co-ordination and the free flow of ideas. Networking addresses these issues and helps organisations work effectively together and spread new ideas and good practice as well as support the career growth and personal development of the individual.

What if we didn't network?

Before we go on to examine the positive reasons for networking, just think about a world in which people didn't network together:

- Ideas would be developed in one part of the business and not allowed to spread to other functions.
- The process of change would be slowed down as new policies moved slowly up and down the chain of command.
- Every job vacancy or place on a working group or task force would have to be the subject of a thorough and time-consuming recruitment process in order to ensure absolute fairness.
- It would be hard to find people of like mind to support you when times got tough.
- Businesses would lack co-ordination or

would be so rigidly co-ordinated that they would lack responsiveness to customer needs.

- Professions would take longer to develop new ideas and innovative ways of working and the sharing of ideas across businesses would be almost non-existent.
- Life would be very boring; we would eat lunch with our closest colleagues at the company canteen and good city restaurants would go out of business.

....

WHAT IS NETWORKING?

A network is simply a group of people linked by a common interest. It is different from a team in that it is usually less structured and is less focused on a particular task or objective. Networks are usually informal and non-hierarchical with status being accorded to members based on their knowledge and their usefulness to others within the network. Some professional networks are more organised than others and formal and informal networks do work quite differently.

Networking is therefore the process of belonging to and operating within a network. 'Networking' is used here to mean any activity that involves working within a network, outside the more formally drawn lines of authority that reside within most large organisations. Some examples of networking activity are:

- going to a meeting of your professional society or institute
- meeting a colleague from another

department for lunch to compare notes on projects which seem to have some overlap

- having lunch with a former colleague who thinks there may be an opening for you in their new company
- talking to a potential client you have met at a conference
- speaking at a professional conference or local meeting of your institute or society
- having a social drink with a friend to talk over some work problems
- browsing the Web in search of new ideas or exchanging ideas in a forum
- attending Round Table, school governors' meetings, Lions, the Chamber of Commerce, or any other organised meeting where you meet other people with different perspectives on life, work and business
- making telephone contact with people who may be interested in your ideas on new products or services.

WHY NETWORK?

Networking is much more than making contacts to help you find new jobs or more business. There are six important reasons for networking – the 6 Cs of networking:

1 Getting things done in a **complex** world

2 Making **connections** for business and life outside business

3 Increasing **creativity** by exchanging ideas with other people

4 Extending your own **continuous development** by learning from other people with different life experiences

5 Increasing your contribution by **collaboration** with others

6 Managing your stress by **collective security** – finding support from others.

Getting things done in a complex world

The world has always been complex but, because of its slower pace, in the past we were able to keep complexity at bay by creating large business and public sector organisations which created the illusion of stability by setting up systems and procedures to ensure that everything worked efficiently. The earlier part of the twentieth century saw the concentration of power within the nation state and the large corporate bureaucracy, the dominant models within the political and economic arena where decisions were made by a few people at the top of an organisation and then pushed through with machine-like efficiency.

Centralised leadership was made possible by technology and the dominant social paradigms of hierarchy, efficiency and stability. Control over the means of communication ensured that the leaders' ideas and strategies monopolised the airways and the prevailing culture of deference ensured the compliance of the majority.

While the technology and the social structure had a disempowering effect during most of the twentieth century, we are now seeing these two factors having the completely opposite effect as we move into the new millennium. As we move from the mainframe to the network, from the centralised to the decentralised and from the national to the global/local business, power is becoming highly diffused and this is radically changing our concept of leadership.

The next century will see leadership and decision making becoming more diffused across our business and governmental organisations. The technological breakthroughs of the last decade coupled with the desire for autonomy and the growing self-confidence of the generations now joining both workforce and electorate mean that our organisations will never be quite the same again, and these new organisations will require not only a different style of leadership but also different assumptions about the way organisations operate.

In the absence of centralised direction, networking will be an important factor in the way people operate in the new organisation. It is the way that organisations and the people within them will cope with the complexity of the new organisational forms – not with formal lines of communication but with managers and professionals making informal links across the organisation – sharing good practice and creating effective processes in support of a broad corporate vision.

Making connections for business and life

The traditional concept of networking is still valid, albeit stripped of the exclusivity and elitism of the past. The idea that people get jobs and contracts through knowing the right people has not changed, although those 'right people' may be a more diverse bunch than they might have been in the past. Making connections with others is one of our best guarantees of future security – what we know and who we know are better protections against insecurity than a cast-iron employment contract.

What we know is our product; *who we know* are our markets – the two together are important factors in our future development. Our connections with others are always critical to success in finding new work or new contracts. Many jobs are filled through the hidden market, both inside and outside organisations, and it pays to know the people who are filling those vacancies. Many organisations have formal selection policies and procedures, indeed equal opportunities legislation makes it a requirement for most jobs. The reality is, however, that managers want to appoint people that they know and trust and so alongside the formal process is an informal process of checking out track record, style and approach – so having some good connections both inside and outside your business is an important factor in your future career growth.

This is important not only for jobs but also for opportunities to go on prestigious working parties or task forces or to gain access to the most useful development opportunities. Developing and using your contacts to identify opportunities for growth is a useful skill to learn as it ensures that you become known to the people who have the authority to make things happen as someone who has ambition and a strong desire to get on. I have worked with many highly competent people who have complained that their careers have been derailed because they weren't known to the top management in their organisations. If it has happened to you, then plan for it not happening again by identifying the key people in your business or profession and ensuring that they know your identity, your track record and your aspirations.

In the wider world of external recruitment, almost all top jobs are filled through search rather than selection. Headhunters work through contacts and if your name isn't on their contact list then it won't be on the short list. Effective networking helps you get on to those lists – not through calling them directly but through knowing the key people in each business or profession who provide the search consultants with contacts and referrals.

Many self-employed people find that a large number of their contracts, particularly in the early days, come from close personal contacts. This is natural – businesses want to work with advisers and suppliers that they can trust and so a recommendation supported by a detailed personal knowledge of a potential supplier is likely to be more powerful than an advert in a local paper or a professional journal or even than a brochure sent through the mail.

Connections are important for your future prosperity but you must start making connections even if you don't feel the need to change at the moment. The aim of networking is to develop good working relationships with people so that they can offer you work or recommend you to others based on a good knowledge of your approach and a high degree of trust. This takes time and so you should start now to build up this network – people are, not surprisingly, cynical about the motives of individuals who suddenly appear looking for a job after redundancy when they haven't seen them for years, or who start to call them after years of silence, just as their new business is getting under way. Networking is for life and not just for Christmas!

Increasing creativity by looking at ideas from others' perspectives

There are two broad types of creativity: 'pure' creativity, the flash of inspiration which comes from nowhere, and 'adaptive' creativity, the adapting or borrowing of ideas from other people or other disciplines. For many of us, the latter is a more productive source than the former as we take ideas from one business or department and use them elsewhere. For both approaches, a diverse network is particularly important to give us access to new ideas and to introduce us to new ways of looking at the same problem.

It is a sad reflection on most business organisations that they benchmark in their own industry and against their main competitors and go no further. By making comparisons against people like themselves, they learn nothing really new and rob themselves of the opportunity to look at their business from a whole new perspective. Networking is a form of benchmarking – we are comparing our own approach to business with that of other people, and the more diverse that group, the more interesting will be the results.

Extending your own continuous development

Creativity and learning are closely related. Exposure to new ideas is an important part of increasing your creativity but networking also helps to spread ideas quickly across a group within an industry or profession.

Arie de Geus talks in his book *The Living Company* about the reasons why blue tits learned to siphon off the cream from milk bottles while robins did not, despite no apparent dissimilarity in the technical ability of individual birds. The keys to the blue tits' success are its social groupings and mobility – blue tits live in flocks, robins are aggressively territorial – and although some robins have been seen taking the tops off milk bottles, they have never learnt to disseminate the process across the whole species. The blue tits have found ways to propagate the skill and thus the whole species has acquired the useful and important skill of taking cream out of milk bottles. 'Birds that flock ... seem to learn faster' concludes the author.

For 'flock' read 'network'. People who have a wide network make contact with a wider range of new ideas and so learn faster. The territorial professional learns nothing new and this is tantamount to career suicide in a fast-moving world. If we look at the speed with which new management ideas spread, it must certainly increase in direct proportion to the increase in conferences and symposia. Short-sighted managers who see only the bottom line costs of such events fail to appreciate the power of internal and external conferences as ways to increase the dissemination of ideas. Conference organisers must resist the temptation to schedule every possible hour for autocued speeches and allow more time for 'flocking' – the informal huddling around the bars and restaurants where real ideas are discussed and exchanged.

Networking is helpful for our own personal development, too. Many young managers have grown and developed through the informal interventions of more experienced colleagues, acting as mentors and coaches, although attempts to formalise this process by appointing formal mentors has not always been as successful – another example of trying to formalise and proceduralise an effective informal process.

GOLDEN RULE 1

Use networking as an important part of your personal development.

Talking to a wide variety of people gives you access to a wider range of experience and also gives you different perspectives on your own experience. Learning from your own experience is useful but it is even more useful to be able to learn from other people's, especially when their experience is wider and more varied than your own.

Learning from experience is not limited to business and professional issues; we also learn from other people's life experience. If we are facing a difficult situation at home or at work, rather than just sitting in our cave and trying to puzzle it out on our own, we should try to find someone who has been through a similar situation and learn from them – not to slavishly follow their every move, but to take the chance to see how other people deal with things, increasing the range of options open to us.

Increasing your contribution by collaboration with others

In the world of corporate strategy, heavy emphasis is put on understanding your business's 'core competencies' and making alliances with other business organisations in order to harmonise with their core competencies and create a more productive and elegant outcome. The principle of focus is supported by a principle of collaboration to ensure that strengths are made productive and weaknesses are managed by finding other organisations with complementary skills.

The same principle applies to individuals – we must focus on the things that we do well and find potential collaborators who can fill in our particular gaps. These collaborators will have strengths in areas different from our own and should be people who we can work with to create a more satisfying result.

This is similar to the key principles of team building, but with networking we move away from the permanent structure of teamwork into a wider frame, seeing everyone as a potential alliance partner or collaborator. Many people who run their own business find it almost impossible to be good at everything – strategy and details, finance and marketing, people and machines, finding business and doing business. They usually need to find someone with different skills and a different approach to fill in the blanks, producing a better overall result for all concerned. This is not limited to the self-employed – many people within large organisations would be more effective at work if they found other people to work with across organisational boundaries to create new and interesting projects.

Managing your stress by collective security

Perhaps the most important reason for networking in this complex and stressful world is that it helps us survive the problems and difficulties in our working lives and our lives outside work. Just talking to people we like and whose company we enjoy is a good antidote to stress. Gathering a support network is an effective way to protect ourselves against the unpredictability of the world and enables us to survive with our self-esteem intact.

The most dysfunctional way to manage stress and solve problems at home and at work is to keep things to ourselves. We have been conditioned – I write as an English middle-class male – to keep our problems to ourselves and to struggle manfully on until we resolve them. The rise of stress related illness shows us that this particular approach is certainly not working and that a less intensive and more relaxed approach may be required.

However, the conventions in our workplace are still against making explicit our concerns and worries – it can still be seen as a source of weakness. The sensible middle way is to find people with good listening skills and a high degree of empathy and talk to them about our work and some of the difficult issues we face. Not as a whinging or griping session, but with someone to whom we can talk openly and honestly without concern that they will be judging or disapproving of us. These people will probably be outside our organisation or in different parts of the business.

Examples of networking

Networking requires a broad set of skills and we embark on a networking campaign in the knowledge that it is for life and it will be one of the most important features of our life in the millennium, both inside work and outside. Before embarking on the campaign, here are some examples of effective networking and networkers.

Tony O'Reilly

In the book *The Player – The Life of Tony O'Reilly*, Ivan Fallon describes making and keeping contacts as an important aspect of O'Reilly's career with Heinz and his own Irish-based business, mixing in very wide circles, holding parties where he brought politicians, business leaders and sporting heroes together. His deputies describe the size and quality of his network – mixing with presidents and prime ministers at one moment but, at a lower level, also knowing the key operators who have the information that he needs to make good business decisions.

Forum UK

A magazine article described Forum UK as one of Britain's most powerful networking groups involving women who are public figures, business leaders, lawyers and other professional leaders. As one member put it: 'There's an instant wealth of connections and ideas here for tapping. And these people are just great fun.' The article describes the group as 'enjoy-(ing) each other's company. They tap into each other's expertise, they cross fertilise ideas and they have a good laugh'. The article might also be describing The National Federation of Women's Institutes, The British Association of Women Police, Women in Property, Women in Journalism, and so on.

Bell Labs

Bell Labs in the USA recognised that a key differentiator between its star researchers and their colleagues was not IQ but was the way that they worked with others including net-working and spreading good practice. The star performers would be less likely to be stumped by technical problems – not just because of their superior technical ability but because they had effective networks in place to get help and advice when they needed it. (For further information, see Robert Kelley's book *Star Performer*.) Daniel Goleman in his book *Emotional Intelligence* sees this as a good exam-ple of the power of high EQ (their Emotional Quotient) working effectively in tandem with high IQ.

SUMMARY

Networking is an important strategy for busi-ness and personal success in the future. The aim of *Powerful Networking* is to demystify and clarify approaches to networking.

Part One examines the concept of networks and the sort of networks that you should belong to and the types of people you should have in your network.

Part Two is based on a questionnaire to discover your own personal networking style.

Part Three focuses on the skills of networking and suggests ways that you can develop them.

Part Four looks at specific networking situations and how to tackle them.

Part Five is an action plan based on the twenty golden rules of networking you will find throughout the book, to get you out networking effectively and able to sustain your networking campaign.

Part one

THE FEATURES OF A GOOD NETWORK

Networks are now seen as one of the features of the new ways of working, although in many ways they are a return to an earlier age. They work quite simply and are a good antidote to the hierarchical world of the large organisation. Many authors on organisational behaviour have noted that an informal network has always underpinned formal organisation structures, which has been an important factor in the way that things have been done around the organisation. The grapevine has always been faster than the formal communication infrastructure – the speed with which a rumour flashes around the business is ten times faster than waiting for the weekly team briefing meeting, which doesn't tell you the really interesting information anyway.

....

HOW NETWORKS WORK

We will examine the different types of network later in the chapter. Networks can be purposeful or spontaneous, but in any case all networks share some important features and these features are the things that differentiate them from the formal hierarchies of large business and public sector organisations. I have identified five features of networks, which help to explain how they work:

1 They are informal and non-hierarchical.

2 They are based on relationships of friendship and trust.

3 They offer open access, free ranging and an easy exit.

4 They are bottom-up – run by the members for their own benefit.

5 Power in a network is based on knowledge and contribution, not status.

Networks are informal and non-hierarchical

Networks are by their nature informal and they often grow up as a response to the ineffectiveness of structured, centralised organisations. We have all grown up in the era of the large organisation and so it is easy to forget that some of the most effective and productive organisations have been based on informal networks with no real central control, although they often have a clear common vision and sense of purpose.

The Internet is a good example of an effective organisation that is based on a network. It is not owned by anyone but is a set of leased lines to connect different private and public networks. There is no controlling mechanism, which is its strength, and one of the reasons for its great success, particularly with a generation that is mistrustful of central control.

Another example is the Visa organisation, owned by over 20,000 financial institutions and processing over 7 billion transactions a year worth $650 billion. Visa itself is only a relatively small overseeing structure *linking its members' operations together to make one of the most influential financial services in the world today.*

Both these networks have found that new ideas and new energies flow from their members not because of a powerful corporate board of directors demanding creativity, but because they emerge naturally. Informality is the key to good networks, not creating committees, procedures and rule books. When dogma takes over, the fun and energy of the network disappear and it becomes more like another day at the office.

Networks are based on relationships of friendship and trust

Because networks are informal and low on hierarchy and procedures, they rely on personal rather than formal relationships. Rosabeth Moss Kanter in her book *World Class* comments that in good business networks, members 'make friends before they make deals'. Before you gain any tangible benefit from a network, you need to have established your personal credibility based on trustworthiness and your value as a friend as well as a business contact.

Some of the most powerful networks in the world are based on national and family ties and they have strict conventions of honour and behaviour (a quite different concept to rules and procedures). The 'Overseas Chinese', people of Chinese origin living outside the borders of Communist China, is the most powerful network in South East Asia and it works on a basis of mutual understanding and respect. Before the recent problems in Asia, it was the third largest economic grouping in the world behind the US and Japan. It runs as a network based on family and ethnic ties but with no central, controlling mechanism.

One of the mistakes of networking is to expect favours and contacts from people before your have established a good personal relationship with them. One of the key principles of networking is that you enter the network one relationship at a time – your first contact will often give you other names and you begin to enter further into the web. To give someone access to your personal network is an act of generosity and one that should not be taken lightly. It is unlikely that this will be done if you are not seen as a trusted member of the network as the introduction of a dysfunctional member of a network can damage the relationships of the original group. This is particularly important in informal, personal networks.

Have you ever introduced someone to a group of your friends and seen the balance of relationships change because of this new member of the group? They may not quite 'fit in', or they might fit in too well and your relationships with the other members of the group change. This can happen with networks – someone with a style or approach that is inconsistent with the dominant group values can damage or destroy the effectiveness of the network.

Every new member introduced to a network can add value by bringing new ideas and new approaches, but they must be trusted and must be respectful of the informal norms of the group. This is why the archetypal 'bull at a gate' business card flashers are often poor networkers, because they are not sensitive to the needs of the others in the network and not prepared to invest the time in building long-term relationships based on mutual trust and reciprocity.

Networks offer open access, free ranging and easy exit

The Internet is an interesting metaphor for the new styles of networking. You need a PC, a modem and a telephone line for access and then you are free to roam the Net at will, leaving when you decide you are ready to leave. The most effective networks are the same, offering easy access without any particular strictures about where to go when you are in the network and permission to leave when you feel ready. The best networks are those where people don't want to leave because they are gaining so much in terms of connections, ideas and personal development.

Networks are there whether you use them or not. Some are established, some are 'virtual' and some are there to be set up – a group of people who have similar interests but have not yet recognised it. If you can't find a network, then set one up. It takes one telephone call or one e-mail to set up a network – you need to talk to one other person and then both begin to contact others with similar needs, interests or approaches. They don't have to be permanent – you can stop your 'membership' of a network at any time, although you probably won't want to if it is giving you useful contacts and new ideas.

They are 'bottom up' – run by their members for their own benefit

Networks have no real 'head', although they may have a centre around which their members organise. Some more formal networks – professional institutions, societies and so on – may have a broad structure as the basis for meetings and communications. These structures are usually based on the principle of subsidiarity – the 'higher' structures and processes are only allowed as much authority as the members are prepared to give them to enable the network to operate successfully.

This 'bottom up-ness' is an important feature of good networks as it means that the functioning of the network is allowed to move flexibly to meet its members' needs rather than to be controlled by a central unit. This means that networks adjust to change very quickly as the decision makers are in constant contact with the real world. Large centralised structures suffer because their decision makers in head office are usually protected from the real world by layers of management; networks are not managed and so, apart from sharing a common purpose and values, they are free to respond to changing circumstances. The Internet is a good example – it has made many small changes since its inception, but these changes have been made by a small group of subscribers and then the new practice has grown as more subscribers see the benefits. Changes are not at the behest of some bureaucrat at Internet HQ.

Power in a network is based on knowledge and contribution, not status

In many organisations, power is largely based on status and position. In networks, power is based on knowledge and contribution rather than status. Knowledge is what you bring to a network – knowledge of ideas, of people, of new sources of information – and is part of the value that you add to a network. Your contribution is your ability to use that knowledge to help and support other people. These factors will bring you power in a network – not political manoeuvring, although you can gain greater influence within a network by recognising and developing your relationship with the key people. Power is not equally distributed within a network but it is more widely distributed than it would be in a more centralised and structured organisation. The principle of easy exit ensures that power is not too easily centralised. Members can vote with their feet if they feel that a network does not meet their needs, and so if there is a formal structure within the network, it must remain sensitive to the needs of its members, otherwise it will quickly lose membership.

WHAT SORT OF NETWORKS CAN YOU BELONG TO?

Networking is a name that we now give to a process that has been going on under different names for years. The guilds in the Middle Ages were professional networks that supported the development of young professionals and provided collective security for craftsmen. Freemasons were such a powerful network in the nineteenth century that they were outlawed in many countries in Europe. Other words that we might use for networking might be 'collaborating', 'associating', 'combining' and 'socialising' – all part of this wider concept of networking.

You probably belong to several networks, some of which you might not recognise as such or call them by that name. In this section, I identify different types of network and discuss where they can be helpful in your career success and your personal development. There are three broad categories, although the boundaries are quite fuzzy and some of your networks may fall into two or more categories:

- personal and social
- professional and occupational
- organisational.

GOLDEN RULE 2

Map out your current network.

Personal and social

The least formal and least structured of your networks will be your personal or social networks. However, your social networks may be the most useful and productive for you over the years. Many people are afraid to cultivate these networks for their career advancement because they feel awkward about using a social relationship for business purposes. Yet your social network will be made up of people with whom you already have a relationship built on trust and mutual respect and affection.

✎ As you read through the following descriptions of personal network sources, for each one write down a list of people who fall into these categories, who you know well and trust and who you believe trust and respect you.

Your education

Friends from school, university and college are an important element of your network. Many academic institutions recognise the importance of networking for their own future survival – setting up student associations and alumni groups and organising reunions and informal get-togethers.

✎ Write down the names of your closest friends when you were at school or college – where are they now? How do you keep in touch?

✎ Does your school and college have alumni groups? They may have newsletters that would enable you to keep up to date with others from your year group, or they may have regional reunions in your locality. They may also have a Web site that you can check for details of alumni activities.

✎ Think back to other school friends whose company you enjoyed – can you get back in touch with them?

Your hobbies and interests

One of the most difficult aspects of networking is finding common ground in order to build rapport. Sharing a common interest or hobby with someone immediately overcomes that barrier. A common interest or a common membership of a social organisation is an easy route towards a more productive relationship. You should try to be as open as possible about your main interests and affiliations when meeting people – you may come across a common interest early in your relationship.

We are often warned about the halo effect in interviewing – the idea that if we share some features with the candidate then we will automatically see them in a more positive light. It is a dangerous phenomenon in selection because it stops us from being objective about the person and may lead us to favour them over a more highly qualified candidate who doesn't share similar interests. It is dangerous because it is so powerful – we do develop rapport more quickly with someone who belongs to the same church or shares our membership of Round Table or the Lions.

It may be wrong for a formal selection event, but it is right for building a good networking relationship. Informal relationships grow more quickly when we find ourselves on the same wavelength as someone we meet. A shared interest is a great help in doing this.

✎ Write down a list of your hobbies, interests, community interests, association memberships and affiliations. Answer these questions:

- Can you become more involved – as an organiser or a more active member?
- What value does your membership add? If it adds value, then develop it; if it doesn't, then you should consider focusing your time on something that is more productive.
- Who are your main contacts in each of your activities? What opportunities are there for increasing your contacts? Are there people who you would like to know better?

✎ Are there other interests that you would like to develop? What would they add to your network?

Remember that interests and hobbies are recreational and that networking should be more for pleasure than profit. Nothing is more counterproductive than blundering into a social event handing out business cards. Your prime purpose in personal networking is to meet new people and to enjoy their company – but also remember that people like to do business with people they know and trust. Make sure that people know your profession and your business interests; do it subtly but with confidence. The person you talk to may not share your interest but they may say: 'Oh, you ought to speak to Carol, I think she's in marketing.' That may lead you to another valuable contact with a ready-made link: 'Carol, my name's John Smith. Peter suggested I talk to you. I understand that you work in marketing and I was wondering if you had any experience of briefing market research agencies … '

Another list to check is your partner's contacts and interests. When I started up my own business, my wife was invaluable in telling people that I was running my own consultancy and her comments led to many good local contacts. You should not put your family under pressure to sell you or your business, but they may be in a good position to make some valuable contacts for you to follow up.

Your family and close friends

Family and friends come into the trusting relationships category. Many cultures focus their business activities around family and close friends because of the need to have complete faith in the integrity of their business partners. Your family can be a good source of support and security but can also be helpful in finding other contacts for you. Referrals from family members can be particularly beneficial as they will normally be supported with great enthusiasm. Parental friends who will normally be a generation ahead of you in the workplace may be able to act as mentors or even be in a position to provide you with an entry into their own workplace networks.

One important caveat: working in the same place as your parents, or a close family member, can be the source of some tensions. However good you are and however hard you work, if you are working for a member of your family, people will always ascribe your successes to nepotism, whether or not this is true. Your family may be the source of uncritical admiration and so their descriptions of your capabilities may be more fulsome than objective.

✎ Write down a list of family and friends who may be in a position to help you.

Current or former work colleagues

Your work colleagues – both present and future – should be an important part of your network. Some organisations – notably the management consultants, McKinsey – formalise this by holding regular events for their alumni, who are a good source of future business for them. There is a great deal of potential reciprocity between former colleagues. They are now in different businesses with different approaches and can share new ideas and ways of working. They can also provide referrals for headhunters and other business colleagues. Work colleagues know each other well in a work setting. This is an important advantage over other areas of your personal network.

✎ List some former colleagues with whom you had a particularly good relationship – ensure that you know their current business or home addresses.

✎ Identify your current work colleagues with whom you have a good relationship – take steps to understand their career aspirations and make sure that they know yours.

• Get together with a group of former workmates and organise a reunion of a former company or department.

A friend of mine organised a reunion of a business that had been taken over twelve

*years previously. He had stayed with the
parent company. Like many others, I had
taken jobs elsewhere. He set up a committee
of friends and we brainstormed a list of
around 200 former colleagues, invited them
to a dinner at a central location, which
around 90 people attended. Many of the
attendees had moved into senior positions
with large organisations. Apart from making
contacts, the evening was a great social
success and will almost certainly be repeated.*

- Organise informal social events for your current
  work colleagues – informal drinks rather
  than formal events are easier to organise
  and more likely to create better working
  relationships. Formal events are too stiff and
  structured for effective networking.
- Ensure that you make new contacts at
  corporate events like conferences and formal
  social events. Don't stay with the same old
  group – you see your close colleagues every
  day but you have fewer opportunities to
  meet colleagues from other departments or
  offices. Personal contact, however brief, is
  many times more effective in building a
  good working relationship then telephone or
  e-mail contact.

People with similar characteristics and sharing similar perspectives

There has been a growth in more formal
networks for women's groups, racial and religious groups and people with similar views on

politics and environmental issues. These are set up to provide mutual support for people in these groups and to counteract the pervasive impact of the white male networks which had such an exclusive effect in the past. These networks can be very powerful both for individual support and for collective security – moving the interests of a whole group forward and removing collective barriers to progress.

✎ Write down your responses to these questions:

- What are the barriers to your career progression? Is there a group which can help you remove those barriers?
- What special groups do you or could you belong to? How would they help you?
- Do you have strong views on political, religious or environmental issues? Is there a network that will help you further those beliefs in concert with other people who share your views?

Belonging to these types of network makes you feel more powerful as it enables you to turn your beliefs into action by associating with like-minded people. It also adds to your network of relationships based on trust and mutual understanding and may lead to other positive outcomes for your career and your personal development. Many people have gained their first experience of leadership in a voluntary or community organisation and it has resulted in their taking on other leadership experiences.

Professional and occupational

Much of our professional development is carried out through membership of a professional institute. Many people join their institutes and then never gain the full benefits because they see membership as passive rather than active. It is not altogether surprising that many people prefer to avoid the activities of their professional bodies. They are often pedantic and rule bound, focusing more on the maintenance of professional protocols than the exchange of exciting new ideas – but, of course, this wouldn't be the case if more of their members would take an active part in the running of the meetings.

Some professional societies are not open to a wide variety of members, preferring to keep membership for qualified people. However, many are opening their doors to interested parties without qualifications and the institution and its members benefit from the introduction of new ideas from people not bound by the conventions of the profession or craft.

There are many opportunities for professional networking:

- professional institutes or societies
- business organisations such as the Institute of Directors and CBI
- local organisations such as Chamber of Commerce and other local initiatives set up by Training and Enterprise Councils (TECs)
- industry forums
- professional conferences
- training courses
- political organisations – both party organisations and 'think tanks' such as Demos

- lectures and presentations from other industries or leading academics or management thinkers.

Professional and business networks are great sources for ideas and your own personal development. You can identify members of organisations with approaches different from your own and follow up your contacts with one-to-one discussions at a later stage. They are also a good source of mentors – experienced members of the profession who are prepared to share some of their expertise with up and coming professionals.

Organisational

Within your current organisation there will be two sorts of structure: the formal structure based on the organisation chart, and the informal networks based on a web of people who share similar values, who trust each other and who help each other get things done. Increasingly, the formal is less effective than the informal structure and, typically, ideas emerge from the informal networks and are 'blessed' or 'signed off' by the formal structure.

The modern workplace is rather like the Palace of Westminster – formal on the surface with rules, procedures and set piece events underpinned by a mass of informal contacts and political activities. The people who base their influence on the formal structure only are missing the point and missing opportunities to further their aims and their careers.

David Krackhardt and Jeffrey R. Hanson in an article for the *Harvard Business Review* (July/August 1993) identified three types of relationship networks within an organisation:

- the advice network – which identifies the prominent players that people in the business go to for advice
- the trust network – which identifies which colleagues share common interests and provide mutual support in a crisis
- the communication network – which reveals the employees who talk about work issues to other people on a regular basis (otherwise known as the grapevine).

An understanding of these networks will help you to get things done effectively within the informal structures of your organisation. A critical question for you is whether you are a part of these networks within your own organisation – do people come to you for advice? Do you feel part of the 'in-group' within your business, or do you sense that there is a lot going on somewhere that you aren't really involved with?

Are you part of an organisational network?

✎ Start by answering the following questions:

- What are your goals in your current role – related both to your current job and to your future career?
- Who is in a position to help you achieve those goals in your current organisation? How well do you know and trust them? How well do they know and trust you?
- How are you perceived by others in your organisation? Do they come to you for

advice? Do they pass information on to you?

- Are you one of the first or one of the last people to know about important changes within the organisation? Where do you get your information from?
- Who do you go to for advice? Who do you trust with confidential information?
- What are the important networks in your department, division or organisation? How close are your links to them? Who are the members and how do you get to meet them?
- Who makes the important decisions in your area of expertise? Who has the veto?

If you don't have the answers to these questions, sit down and draw yourself a map of your organisation. List the key relationships you need to have and then identify ways to develop them. This is a process that will require both boldness (in making the initial contact) and subtlety (in making the right approach in the right way) and you should work on the comfort zones of the people you want to approach. We will look at the skills of building and developing relationships later in the book, but for now just list the key relationships you want to initiate or develop.

The wider organisational networks

Increasingly, the boundaries of organisations are becoming fuzzier and so don't forget to develop networks across organisational boundaries with:

- suppliers
- customers

- other divisions or businesses within your own organisation
- other members of your profession in other parts of the organisation
- joint venture partners and alliances
- regulators or government bodies
- competitors or potential competitors
- trade associations
- people in other departments who are doing interesting things, particularly members of strategic task forces or working groups.

Networking within your organisation is not just to win friends and influence people – it is to enhance the flow of new ideas and to learn new things. It is also about developing long-term relationships based on trust and mutual understanding that will be a source of support for the rest of your working life.

WHAT ARE THE FEATURES OF A GOOD NETWORK?

You should have already clarified the importance of networking and the sorts of networks that you can and probably do belong to. The rest of this part of the book analyses the type of people who should figure in a comprehensive and balanced network. Networking is much more than finding and using people who can help you in your career or in helping you find business contacts. You need to have relationships with a wide range of people who can help you in many different ways:

- Gatekeepers – people who have a wide

variety of contacts and who can give you access to other people or other organisations.

- Business finders – who can help you identify jobs or business opportunities.
- Mentors – who will give you advice, support and feedback.
- Soul mates – whose company you enjoy and who give you support and encouragement.
- Role models – who have done what you are thinking of doing and may be prepared to give you advice and guidance.
- Influencers – with authority and seniority who have the clout to make things happen for you and to introduce you to a network at a higher level.
- Coaches – bosses from whom you can learn specific skills and who are enthusiastic delegators.
- Catalysts – who make you think creatively and who give you access to new ideas.
- Complementary partners – with different sets of technical and personal skills to yours and who work together to develop a new service for your business.
- Protégés – who are on their way up in your business; the people with new ideas and fresh perspectives.
- Provocateurs – who can provoke and stimulate you to look at things in a different way.
- One further network you should develop is your virtual network – a group of figures who you can consult on an imaginary basis. Appoint a fantasy board of directors to help you run your 'business'.

As well as people you should seek out, there are some people you should avoid:

- Stress carriers – people who drain you of energy and optimism.
- Cynics – people who tell you that a thing can't be done when what they mean is that they couldn't do it!
- Competitors – people who may have very similar aspirations and who might block your own plans in order to further their own ambitions.

GOLDEN RULE 3

Develop a broad network of people who can support you in different ways.

Gatekeepers

Networks are complex things – they criss-cross and grow like a spider's web. There are some people who stand at the intersection between different parts of the network or between different networks. These people are very influential and will be trusted and respected by the members of different networks. They are known as gatekeepers because they are the people who give you access to networks (or, more crucially, can deny you access). They assess whether an individual is worthy of an introduction to a network and how they can add value to its existing members.

If a trusted gatekeeper acts as a sponsor for you, then you will have saved much time and effort because their seal of approval will open many other doors automatically for you. Identifying the gatekeepers within each network is an important way to manage your networking time and increasing the return on your investment. You must handle these people carefully, however, as their influence can work in two ways. If they believe in you and your value, they will be a strong and effective protagonist. If they are unsure of you and your motives they can effectively bar your way into their networks.

You will recognise gatekeepers quite easily with a little careful research. Depending on the sort of network you are approaching, listen to people in the organisation or society. Who do they talk about and whose opinions seem to carry the most weight? Observe meetings or conferences – who are the people who are listened to? This will indicate respect for their expertise and trust in their integrity. Ask people to recommend a good person to talk to on a particular topic. Within your organisation, identify the people who are always on the key working parties or strategy groups. Within your circle of friends, who do people go to for advice? If the gatekeepers are respected and they respect you, then your credibility will automatically increase with minimal effort on your part.

Manage your approach to these people carefully. Ensure that you understand their needs and the norms and conventions of the network or group that you wish to join. You must work on their comfort zones and not do anything to suggest that you will damage the delicate structure of the network. Be prepared to identify what value you bring to the group and not just think about what value they can be to you. Networking is a reciprocal process where you must give more than you receive.

✎ Answer these questions:

- Who are the gatekeepers in the various networks you belong to?
- How should you approach them? How will you make the first contact?
- What value can you add to them?
  Don't just ask what your network can do for you; ask what you can do for your network.

Business finders

While it is important not to overstate the instrumental side of networking, nevertheless an important part of building a business network is to identify people who can help you find new business opportunities or a new job. This may be more difficult than some other networking activities for two reasons:

- you are asking for something quite specific from the other person
- you may need to target someone specifically to get the right sort of new business opportunity.

Identifying people who can help you find a job or a new business opportunity must be done with care.

First, you need to have a clear idea of the sort of opportunity you are looking for and the likely contribution that this individual can make. It is important not to approach people with a vague hope that they can do something for you. This is particularly important if they are a gatekeeper of a substantial network –

with a clear idea of your objectives, they can steer you in exactly the right direction; with the wrong idea they can send you to the wrong contacts; with a very vague idea, they may dismiss you as someone who is not worth dealing with.

Second, clarify in your own mind what is different about you and your capabilities. Don't sell yourself short and try to make a positive impact by describing your 'product offering' with confidence and enthusiasm. Before this sort of discussion, you should have prepared your initial explanation of your capabilities and aspirations, so that you are not stumbling for words. Equally you want to avoid appearing too slick and rehearsed.

Third, identify what you can do to help them. Reciprocity is an important factor in networking and it is important to think through any possible ways in which you can help the other party – perhaps you have access to information that they might find useful, you may have contacts that help them, or you may have some expertise that would help them in a project that they are working on.

Fourth, follow up your meeting with a brief note and follow through quickly on anything that you agreed to do.

Mentors

Everyone Needs a Mentor is the title of a very good book by David Clutterbuck. It is hard to disagree with the sentiment except to add that many of us need more than one. You might want to find different mentors for different elements of your working life:

- a professional mentor who can help you

develop better skills in your chosen
profession
- a mentor within your current organisation
  to help you understand the prevailing
  culture and politics
- 'life mentor' – an older friend or family
  member who can give you help and
  advice in the different stages of your life.

Sports professionals have different coaches for
different aspects of their careers – personal
trainers, motivational coaches, technical
coaches – no one person is uniquely qualified
to act as a mentor in every aspect of your
working life.

Some organisations set up formal mentoring
schemes as part of the development of high
fliers. Mentoring is too subtle to become a
process or a scheme and though some
schemes were successful, others faded through
lack of interest. Effective mentoring depends
on the relationship between the mentor and
their protégé and this is better done by mutual
selection rather than as a compulsory human
resource process.

Try to find someone who can act as a
mentor for you in different parts of your life.
They need not always be particularly senior in
an organisation but it helps if they are both
experienced and sensitive to your needs.
A good mentor should have the following
attributes:

- They should be good listeners and
  observers – able to understand your needs
  and to identify the right time to
  intervene in your career development.
- They should be able to tolerate you doing
  things differently from how they did or
  do them and not impose their own

solutions on your problems.

- They should have enough life experience to be able to put your problems into context, but they do not need to be particularly senior or successful themselves.
- They should be sufficiently objective to be able to give you hard advice and constructive feedback when required but with enough sensitivity to do it in a way that protects your self-esteem.

✎ Answer these questions about mentors for yourself:

- Who are the people who you respect and trust?
- How can you work with them to enter into a mentoring relationship with them?
- What aspects of your work do you find most difficult?
- Who do you know who can help you develop that area more effectively?

Soul mates

Life is difficult and can be stressful. Sometimes we just need to spend time with a compatible friend and talk to them about our work. Somebody who will celebrate our successes and put our failures into context. One of the best remedies for stress is a friend who will not challenge us or give us advice but will listen to us without analysing or judging what we are or what we have done.

Sometimes, soul mates get missed off the list

of networking partners because we think too much about our job, our career and how we should be influencing people in authority. We feel under pressure always to be doing something useful or purposeful and so the pleasures of enjoying a joke over a drink or a meal move further down the list of our priorities. Developing good relationships with people can be entirely purpose free; it becomes an end in itself. Build in some time with your soul mates by doing the following:

- Make a list of people whose company you enjoy for its own sake.
- Try to meet up with one of them once a week; ensure that they remain on your networking list.
- Keep at least one lunch-time free a week for a fun meeting with friends or people at work who you really like – even if you are busy. If you are so busy that you can't spare an hour for your own relaxation during your working week, then you need to look carefully at your time management or your working environment.
- Use the telephone or postcards to keep in touch – a brief chat can work wonders during a stressful day.

Role models

A recent newspaper article on the decline of standards in young men commented on the absence of good role models. Role models are important for us all and help inspire us to do new things and to break out of our comfort zones. If you are planning to make some changes in your life – look for a new job, start working for yourself or make a major career change – then it is important to have some role models in your network.

A role model can tell you what something is really like – they can explain how things work in a different environment and can help guide your first few steps into a new experience. The best person to tell you about climbing Everest is the person who has just been photographed with a flag on the summit – they can talk about their preparations, their feelings and possible pitfalls.

Be careful, however, because your role models will be different from you and while their goals may be similar they may have started from a different point and they will have different strengths and weaknesses from you. Use their experience as a guide and not a template – use their advice carefully but don't follow it slavishly.

✎ Answer these questions:

- What important change do you want to make in your life at the moment?
- Who do you know who has made this change? How can you get to meet them?
- What can you learn from them? How else can you learn about their approach?

Influencers

At the beginning of the list of possible networkers, we looked at gatekeepers, people who, because of their pivotal position in a series of networks, could give you access to a wide range of other contacts. A similar function is fulfilled by the influencers. Influencers are people who can provide you with contacts or leverage by virtue of their own authority and position. Influencers are usually people in senior positions who have the clout to make things happen for you at high levels in an organisation. They will often be good gate-keepers and hold strategic positions in networks – often networks beyond your own level of authority.

Their name will have the same impact that the 'By Royal Appointment' sign has on tourists in Britain. It confers cachet by association and creates a promise of your potential value and quality. This group is not an essential part of your network but it can be a useful addition. High level authority figures do have an advantage in that their approach may often be more long term and strategic. They may be able to add a perspective to your thinking that some of your closer colleagues may not be able to add. I once spent some time with the chairman of a large retail business who gave me several insights into the sort of human resource consultancy work that he felt added real value – this was helpful to me and gave me several positive ideas that I subsequently used in developing my own business.

One warning – senior people are often very sure of their judgement and will probably want to tell you what you should be doing with your life. You may have to resist their forceful attempts to run your life, but if you get the opportunity to meet someone who can open doors at a senior level, then certainly prepare carefully for the meeting – it is most important to have a clear description of your goals and aspirations. If you can think of something that you can do in return for their support, offer to do it.

Coaches

There is a fine line to be drawn between coaching and mentoring. Coaching is the more hands-on day-to-day management of an individual's performance and development; mentoring is a more distant process. The point of including coaches in your network is the importance of maintaining a good relationship with your current and previous bosses.

Your relationship with your boss is one of the most critical that you make at work. If you have a 'good' boss – one who sets you clear goals and gives you objective and accurate feedback on your performance and development – you should ensure that you build a strong and positive relationship with them and do all you can to maintain that relationship in the future, even if you leave the organisation. Good managers are hard to come by and you should work hard to develop the relationship.

Coaching does not come solely from your line manager. Leaders of project teams, 'functional' bosses and other key line managers may also be in a position to provide you with effective coaching. Coaching is a process which involves the gradual development of capability and contribution over a period of time and is particularly important for your continuous development. There is no reason why a good coach should stop just because you no longer work for them – provided they understand your aspirations and provided you take the initiative to engage them in a continuing networking relationship.

✎ Answer these questions to think about possible coaches for yourself.

- Where have you learned the most at work? Who did you work for at that time?
- Which manager did you respect the most and which one seemed to understand you the best?
- Where are your former managers now? How could you keep in touch with them?
- How can you develop your relationship with your current manager? How can you ensure that you get the feedback and support that you need to achieve your career goals?

Catalysts

Exposure to new ideas is an important reason for networking. Jack Cohen, the founder of the Tesco superstore chain, used to say 'You don't do business sitting on your arse', and this could be a good, if rather indelicate, motto for networking. He might also have said 'You don't get ideas from sitting in your office'. Meredith Belbin in the development of his team roles concept, noted that there were two types of creativity: 'pure' creativity, as developed by the plant – thinking up new ideas to solve problems – and 'adaptive' creativity, as demonstrated by the resource investigator – a more extroverted creativity, borrowing ideas from a wide range of people.

The adaptive creative type is usually a good

networker, meeting people and gaining new insights into problems and opportunities before bringing them back to their own team and seeing how they might fit their own set of problems. This sharing of good practice is what makes modern businesses tick and what refreshes the organisation's stock of new ideas. Sometimes the ideas are brought in from outside the organisation, sometimes they are spread across the organisation.

The Bell Laboratories example, referred to earlier, was an excellent case study of the increase in effectiveness that networking could bring to a research centre.

The Bell Laboratories case study

Robert Kelley and Janet Caplan did research to identify the difference between star performers and the average worker at the Bell Laboratories Switching Systems Business Unit. Their research revealed that the real difference between stars and the average researcher wasn't IQ but the way they carried out their jobs. One aspect was their definition of networking – the high performers had networks in place to help resolve technical problems promptly, whereas the average performers either tried to resolve the issue themselves or wasted time waiting for other technical specialists to call back. The star performers found that their networking led to a significant increase in their productivity. They defined networking as 'getting direct and immediate access to co-workers with technical expertise and sharing your own knowledge with those who need it'.

Everyone needs a catalyst in their network – someone who suggests new ideas or who sparks new and original thoughts in you. Some creativity is no doubt caused by flashes of insight, but much more is likely to result from the free exchange of ideas and concepts between departments and across businesses and industry sectors. The effective catalyst says 'Why not do this ... ?' or 'We've tried this way of doing things ... ' or 'Have you ever tried ... ?'. They need a strong sense of curiosity and an openness to giving out their ideas as well as borrowing other people's. So too must you – the reciprocity angle again – the Bell Labs' definition included sharing as well as acquiring technical expertise.

✎ Answer these questions:

- Who do you know who always has new ideas and is aware of the latest techniques and approaches?
- Where do you feel stuck at the moment – where could you do with some new thinking?
- Where might you find those new ideas – not just in your current organisation but in other industries or in other activities?
- Who do you spark with at work? Who always gives you some interesting ideas?

Complementary partners

An increasingly common business strategy is the development of core competencies and the formation of alliances with other organisations possessing complementary skills to create a new product or service. The aim is to make their strengths more productive by making an alliance with another organisation with skills which are different yet complementary. Networking enables organisations and people to focus on their main strengths while finding another person or entity who can help them leverage those strengths by finding new skills and new ways of working.

When two businesses combine their technical expertise, they create a product which is greater than they could develop by working individually. For example, Tesco Stores is working with the Royal Bank of Scotland in the development of a range of financial services products – harnessing the banking skills of the Bank of Scotland with the customer service and marketing skills of Tesco.

This sort of alliance can be carried out in microcosm in your own organisation. How can you combine your professional and managerial skills with someone else to develop an idea that may improve the way your organisation does business? Most large organisations seem to be organised around silos with little movement across them but plenty of movement up and down them. Some possible examples of co-ordination across business functions may be:

- sales and operations combining to improve production planning
- marketing and human resources working together to improve the organisation's understanding of its customers
- finance and distribution combining to develop an improved stock handling process.

Look around your organisation and you will find that most of the business problems occur at the 'hand off', where one part of the organisation passes work over to another.

Effective collaboration can take place between organisations within the supply chain. Working together with your counterparts in your customer's organisation or one of your suppliers can be very productive and you should see your network extend beyond your own organisation into the other businesses.

✎ How can you work with others? Answer these questions:

- Where are the biggest problems in your organisation? How can you help resolve them by increasing cross-functional communication?
- Where can you add value to your customer proposition? Who could you work with in your customers' businesses to improve relations and business?
- What issues are you facing in your current role? Who can you find to work with in your organisation?

Protégés

Many writers put emphasis on what the protégé can learn from the mentor but less on what the more experienced professional can learn from the rising star. Most of us acknowledge that every meeting with a good coach should enable a young professional to learn something, but we forget that the coach should learn something from every meeting with their team.

Our organisations, and indeed our society, has been based on the assumption that the older you get the more experienced and wise you become. This makes sense in a stable world where the longer you live and work the more you understand about the world. It is less valid in a world which is changing rapidly from the bottom up and the executive at the top of an organisation may learn about the changes from the up-and-coming professionals who are closer to the changing environment.

The saddest of figures in corporate life is the dinosaur, desperately clinging on to the old ways of working and basing their decisions on the old assumptions. The antidote to this is to ensure that you keep contact with young and emerging talents within your organisation. They can learn from your life experience and you can learn from seeing the world through their eyes. Keeping up to date and fresh is an important element in enduring career success and one way to do this is to include some potential protégés in your network.

Picking the right person to work with is rather like picking undervalued stocks in the stock market. Identifying people with potential to grow, with the intellect and drive to be successful, can be a productive strategy in your approach to networking.

✎ Which protégés could you invite into your network? Answer these questions:

- Which of your current contacts seem to have some good new ideas and a clear view

of the future in your business/profession?
- Who do you see in your industry or profession who shows real potential for the future? What can you learn from them? How can you help them?

Provocateurs

An earlier category referred to catalysts – people who can introduce you to new ideas and stimulate new thinking. An extension of this category are provocateurs – people who can provoke and stimulate you into thinking the unthinkable and challenge you to move beyond your comfort zone into new and unfamiliar territory. Some of the functions of a provocateur may be:

- to make you see the world from a different perspective
- to challenge you to go beyond your current thinking and to be bolder and more imagintive in your approach to your work
- to introduce you to new and radical ideas from other professions or disciplines
- to stop you taking yourself too seriously.

Whereas most of the other members of your network should be people whose company you enjoy and with whom you feel comfortable, the provocateurs should make you feel a little uncomfortable, should be making you question your current approach to life and should stimulate and provoke you rather than soothe and calm you. This is particularly

important the more senior you become –
someone to fulfil the role of court jester,
pricking the pomposity of the king.

✎ Get ideas for people who can act as
provocateurs by answering these
questions:

- Who do you know who makes you feel
  uncomfortable and yet helps you see things
  from a different perspective?
- Who do you know who has radical new
  ideas on different topics? How can you use
  their ideas to make you think differently
  about your work?
- Which of your current contacts has a
  background and approach to life different
  from yours?

These categories should all be counted within
your network. Some people will fulfil dual or
triple roles for you – acting as mentor, provocateur and gatekeeper for example. Go
through your list of contacts and see how they
fit into different roles.

Your virtual network

The final category for your network is the
virtual network of imaginary figures whose
experience is available for you to consult when
you have a problem or you are faced with an
opportunity. Read widely about great political,
military or sporting figures and then use their
experience to help you through difficulties.

If you have to face a challenge, then imagine how Liz McColgan or John Harvey-Jones would face it. If you are taking a risk, how would Tony O'Reilly or John Hume operate? If your beliefs are threatened – think how Margaret Thatcher or Alex Ferguson would respond. You have access through the media to the thoughts and feelings of a wide range of successful people. These can help stimulate you to think carefully about your own issues at work and at home.

✎ Think about the following:

- Who do you admire? What lessons have you learned from them?
- What situations are you facing at the moment? What famous people have faced similar issues? What can you learn from them?
- How can you find out more about your potential role models?

Who should not be in your network

There are some types who should not figure in your network. Try to identify people who fit into these categories and spend less time with them.

GOLDEN RULE 4

Avoid networking with people who drain you of energy.

Stress carriers

Some people suffer from stress and some seem immune to it but carry it to other people. People who bring stress into your life are best ignored and where possible isolated where they do less harm. A few people who fit into this category are those who:

- whinge and moan but do little to change things
- rush around creating panic but have few ideas to resolve things
- involve you in endless projects of their own and then don't support your own
- complicate or confuse things.

Cynics

Cynics can be a corrosive influence on people who are looking to grow and develop. They tell you things can't be done and criticise you for trying to change things. They are usually people who complain about their lot but lack the courage to make the necessary changes. They try nothing new but block anyone else who is trying to make changes.

It takes a lot of energy to get round a cynic and it usually isn't worth trying; far better to keep that energy for the positive issues that you face at work. It is often more useful to go round a blockage than to move it out of the way.

Competitors

Be careful about talking too much about your plans and aspirations to people who might wish to frustrate them. This doesn't mean that you should ignore competitors – in fact, you may find that they are similarly ambitious people and you may identify a strong sense of common purpose with them. The care is required in telling them too much about your own personal goals and aspirations as this may encourage them to frustrate or work against them.

✎ Do you have people in your network who fall into the categories of stress carrier, cynic or competitor?

....

SUMMARY

The size, scope and composition of your network is a personal decision. This chapter will have helped you identify what you want from your networks, and people you would like to include in them. Your network is unlikely to be as tidy and organised as I have suggested, but you certainly need to have a wide range of members, both real and virtual, within your network, in order to develop and refresh your ways of working and to grow your career in the direction that you desire.

The next chapter will examine your style and approach to networking before moving on to identify the important skills and techniques.

WHAT KIND OF NETWORKER ARE YOU?

Before examining some of the skills and techniques of networking, it will be useful for you to examine your own style and approach. One of the golden rules is to understand your own personal style so that you are never operating in a way that feels unnatural and false. There are two key issues that we will consider:

- your prime interest in networking
- your natural orientation.

We will identify your natural approach first and then examine ways in which you can develop other approaches that feel natural and unforced. The third part of the book covers the skills of networking; part Two will help you analyse the skills that are most important to you.

....

YOUR NETWORKING APPROACH

The following activity is not a psychometric test but is intended to get you to think broadly about yourself and where you feel most comfortable. Knowing your comfort zone is an important starting point in any activity, but it is equally important for your personal development to know how to stretch your comfort zone and to keep extending it.

✎ For each of the following scenarios there are four networking approaches that you are most likely to take in each situation. For each scenario allocate a total of ten marks among the given options that you think would best describe your reaction (you may allocate an option zero if you wish). There are no right or wrong answers as each alternative is a perfectly valid and reasonable approach to take. At the end of the exercise, you will simply identify which of four broad networking types most accurately reflects your own style and approach.

How would you approach ...

Scenario one – the reunion

You have been invited to a reunion of a business that you worked in several years ago. The reunion includes a wide range of people invited from across the business. Some of the people who are there will be from your old department, there will be some senior people who have since moved on to bigger and better things, and several people who you probably won't know from other departments. Which of these four categories of people are you most likely to spend most of your time with?

MARK

1   The senior people, because they can make high level connections for you and are in a good position to make things happen for you in the business world   _____

2 Your old friends, because you enjoyed their company so much when you worked together _____

3 Some completely new people from another department who seem like an interesting bunch and have a lot of good ideas _____

4 Some of your old bosses and mentors, because you learned so much from them _____

TOTAL 10

Scenario two – the institute committee

You are approached to stand for election to the regional committee of your local professional institute. You have been a regular, if spasmodic, attendee over the years and you feel that you should get more involved. There are four committee roles that you could consider. Which would you prefer?

MARK

1 Chair of the Professional Development Committee _____

2 Member of the Institute 2005 project which is researching best practice in new technical developments within the Institute _____

3 Chairman of the subcommittee organising the social calendar _____

4 Vice-chair of the region with special responsibility for business development _____

TOTAL 10

Scenario three – the dinner party

You are away on a long-term business secondment overseas and one of your new colleagues invites you to a dinner party. What sort of people do you most hope to meet?

MARK

1   Unconventional people with
    new and exciting ideas   _____

2   Influential people in business or
    the professions who can help
    you establish yourself in the
    local business community   _____

3   People whose company you
    will enjoy and who can make
    your stay more congenial   _____

4   Intellectuals who can teach you
    something about the history
    and culture of your new
    location   _____

                               TOTAL   10

Scenario four – the new job

You have just started work in a new organisation. You have moved house and are working in an industry which is new to you. What sort of people will you seek out in the early days of your induction?

MARK

1   The people with their eyes on
    the future development of the
    business   _____

2 Possible coaches and mentors
   to help you learn more about
   the organisation and its culture _____

3 Good friends and congenial
   work-mates _____

4 The senior people with
   authority to make things
   happen for you _____

                                    TOTAL 10

Scenario five – a figure in authority

You have managed, after much persistence, to get an appointment to meet a leading figure within your industry, who is also a well-known public figure. You have a relatively brief appointment and so you have to clarify your personal objectives. Which of these issues will have the highest priority?

                                        MARK

1 A discussion about the key
   trends in the industry _____

2 A better understanding of the
   skills that will be important for
   the future _____

3 An opportunity to gain their
   support for some of your own
   projects and future plans _____

4 The development of a positive
   working relationship and a
   better understanding of their
   personal needs _____

                                    TOTAL 10

Scenario six – working in a specialist area

You are a professional working in a large laboratory with over 300 technical and professional people, engaged in a series of unrelated projects. The projects are from different clients and while they may have some technical similarities, they have quite different outcomes. The HR manager suggests a series of professional development meetings and conducts a questionnaire to identify what people want to get from the events. Which of these objects are most likely to attract you?

MARK

1   To improve working relationships across the laboratory   _____

2   To improve opportunities for career advancement   _____

3   To spread good practice and increase the circulation of good ideas   _____

4   To learn new techniques and develop new skills   _____

TOTAL   10

Scenario seven – attending a conference

You are due to attend a conference on 'Empowerment', a topic with which you are not very familiar. You are deputising for your boss and have had no opportunity to get a set of objectives from her. What sort of objectives will you set yourself?

MARK

1   To learn some new techniques that you can use in your normal working life   _____

2   To meet some interesting people and enjoy the event   _____

3   To make some useful contacts to help you in advancing your career   _____

4   To identify the leading edge thinking in this area   _____

TOTAL   **10**

Scenario eight – a chance meeting

You are introduced to a stranger at a drinks party. You find out that they work in a similar profession to you. What are your first thoughts?

MARK

1   Who do they know and how can they help me?   _____

2   What can I learn from them?   _____

3   Will I get on with them?   _____

4   What are their views on some new techniques within the industry?   _____

TOTAL   **10**

Scenario nine – an internal business meeting

You are the chairman of a cross-functional task force in your organisation. You convene the first meeting. What will your objectives be for the meeting?

		MARK
1	An assessment of current best practice across the organisation and in the industry as a whole	_____
2	A statement of the business objectives of the task force	_____
3	The members of the team getting to know each other	_____
4	A discussion about the team's process and how the team should learn from the process	_____

TOTAL   10

Scenario ten – your work motivation

You enjoy work more when you are:

		MARK
1	Achieving stretching goals	_____
2	Learning new things and developing as a person	_____
3	Working with leading edge ideas and concepts	_____
4	Working with congenial people in a pleasant atmosphere	_____

TOTAL   10

....

YOUR NETWORKING TYPE

 To establish the type of networking most appropriate for your style and approach transfer your marks from the exercise on the previous page into the grid on the next page against the option number in each row.

You should now have a set of scores against four approaches to networking – business, relationships, ideas, learning – which will give you a sense of your favoured approach and your most important networking priorities. This is not a psychological test but it is a way to get you thinking about your preferred networking style. The four types need to be explained in more detail and the following notes will help you to see the important issues involved in each approach. In reality, of course, you may have a range of approaches to networking depending on the situation and this is the most flexible and productive strategy.

As you examine the different aspects of networking, think about where you feel more comfortable and where you need to develop new skills or to push yourself out of your comfort zone. For example, you may be good at building warm working relationships but need to steel yourself to carry out a more focused and transactional form of deal making.

The following summaries are based on a strong preference for a particular style of

Scenarios

	One	Two	Three	Four	Five	Six	Seven	Eight	Nine	Ten	TOTAL
Business	1	4	2	4	3	2	3	1	2	1	
Relationships	2	3	3	3	4	1	2	3	3	4	
Ideas	3	2	1	1	1	3	4	4	1	3	
Learning	4	1	4	2	2	4	1	2	4	2	

networking. You should balance the comments for less distinct preferences.

Understand your own personal networking style.

Business

Business types are networkers who have a good eye for a deal and are keen to find contacts who can help them further their business or career. They have a clear focus on what they want to achieve and will set clear objectives for their networking meetings. They are more comfortable in the more transactional style of networking, preferring to focus on business issues and tasks rather than building long-term networking relationships.

The potential weakness with the business networking style is that individuals focus so clearly on their own objectives that they are less able to think about the goals and aspirations of their networking partners. Their focus is on short-term results rather than on building a long-term relationship and they can appear to be using people rather than building a relationship for its own sake. They will concentrate on the outcomes of a networking meeting rather than the process and may drop network partners when they feel that they have squeezed enough from them.

Business networkers' strengths are:

- they have clear objectives for their networking campaign and for each meeting
- they are alert for opportunities to further

their career and their business interests
- they are quick to make connections and to get down to the business of the discussion.

They usually need to develop:

- the ability to develop and sustain long-term relationships
- a stronger sense of reciprocity in a relationship
- a greater degree of empathy for the needs and interests of others.

Relationships

Networkers with a strong relationship style are normally effective at building rapport and developing a good understanding of other people's needs and aspirations. They see the networking relationship as just that – a relationship – and will put more emphasis on the process of networking than its outcomes. They are good at supporting and mentoring, although they may avoid challenging their partners because of their strong need to avoid conflict.

Relationship types find the initial stages of the networking relationship difficult to sustain because of their need to avoid imposing themselves on a potential networking partner. They may also start a meeting in a rather unstructured way as they prefer to build rapport based on personal style rather than get straight down to business. They will be good reciprocators as they will not want to see the relationship damaged by a perception of one-sidedness.

Relationship networkers' strengths are:

- building rapport with their contacts and

developing a strong relationship based on empathy
- developing and building long-term relationships
- keeping in touch with their networking partners on a personal as well as a business basis.

They normally need to develop:

- a boldness about approaching people without appearing to impose on them
- a crisp start to any networking meeting with clear objectives and a precise agenda
- better political and influencing skills so that they have a greater impact on situations and people.

Ideas

Ideas types are particularly interested in net-working to gain access to new ideas and to gain some fresh perspectives on their current or future issues. They enjoy meeting new people from different fields and are more likely to network outside their normal field as they will be following up particular ideas and concepts. They will establish 'intellectual' rap-port quickly as they will talk about their current interests and ideas very readily.

Some ideas types can get caught up in their ideas to such an extent that they don't extend their rapport building to other people's more practical needs, particularly their emotional needs, which they may see as subordinate to the realm of ideas. They will have quite clear objectives about the meeting but will be less crisp in managing the relationship or in iden-tifying necessary actions that arise from the discussion.

Ideas networkers' strengths are:

- they are quick to understand other people's intellectual or technical interests, especially when they coincide with their own
- they will sustain long-term relationships with like-minded people
- they will be able to influence others by the power of their ideas.

They normally need to develop:

- a stronger sense of other people's emotional and practical needs
- clarity of purpose in putting their ideas to practical use
- the ability to invest in the process of the relationship and not just the intellectual content.

Learning

Learning types will invest in networking in order to maximise their personal and professional development. They will have a strong drive for continuous development and will look to identify the learning in most situations. They are as interested in other people's learning as their own and they may start to approach their networking relationships like a series of seminars. They will explain concepts carefully and will probably follow up their meetings with notes and relevant articles. They will prove effective mentors and coaches, provided they learn to be crisper and more challenging to other people.

Learning types may suffer from a lack of crispness in the transactional elements of the meetings and of the wider relationship. They may also find it more difficult to clarify objectives for meetings beyond the developmental aspects.

Learning networkers' strengths are:

- they are good as mentors and keen to derive the most learning from any situation
- they will build rapport quickly with people of a similar orientation but are less likely to do so with others
- they are a good source of support and information.

They usually need to develop:

- a greater interest in the business outcomes of the meeting
- a greater awareness of when to coach and when not to
- an alertness to opportunities to further their career or their business interests.

How effective are your meetings?

These pen pictures are indicators of types and possible style issues and should not be seen as stereotypes. You should spend some time analysing your networking style and you can use this simple format as a way to check the effectiveness of your meetings. Ask yourself:

- What were my objectives going into the meeting and how were they achieved?
- How has the relationship grown and developed as a result of the meeting? Do both parties feel that they are gaining from it?
- What new ideas have I learned? How might I use these in my own work?
- What did I learn from the meeting and what did the other person learn?
- What is my style and what is the style of the other person?

....

EXTROVERT OR INTROVERT?

A further spin that needs to be put on your networking style is the difference between extroversion and introversion. Extroverts are literally facing outwards towards the world; introverts spend more time turned in towards themselves.

 Answer the following questions by underlining the alternative that is more indicative of your typical behaviour:

Column A	**Column B**
Enjoys meeting new people	Prefers well-established contacts
Alert to new opportunities	Absorbed in own thoughts
Confident in social situations	Slower to respond in social situations
Communicates best by talking	Communicates best by writing
Wide range of relationships	Fewer, deeper relationships
Takes the initiative in relationships	Slow to initiate relationships
Seeks visibility	Private and reserved
More interested in people than ideas	More interested in ideas than people
Enjoys social gatherings	Happy with own company
Generates new ideas by talking to others	Generates new ideas by reflecting alone

If you underlined more from column A than column B then your networking style is more likely to be extroverted than introverted. This means that you are more likely to be comfortable with the process of making connections with other people and taking the initiative in networking relationships. Introverts can be very effective networkers but may need to learn some skills to enable them to find a way into a networking relationship; once in, however, they are likely to be as effective as extroverts and possibly more so in developing deeper and longer-lasting relationships.

Combining both concepts gives us a set of eight approaches, which can be characterised as shown in the matrix.

Extroverted business type	**Introverted business type**
• Proactive and energetic in making contacts with others • Focused approach with clear objectives • Transactional approach – not a long-term relationship	• Less confident in making initial contact • Focused on own objectives, less so on others' • Once the contact is established, may form long-term business relationship
Extroverted relationship builder	**Introverted relationship builder**
• Warm and friendly with wide range of contacts • Makes connections and builds rapport quickly and easily • Network is more wide than deep	• Slow to make initial contact and possibly hesitant in early stages • Builds rapport slowly but surely – less open in the early phases • Network is more deep than wide

Extroverted ideas gatherer	Introverted ideas gatherer
• Develops ideas by talking to others • Many contacts from a wide range of business sectors • Regular attendance at meetings and conferences	• Generates ideas by reflecting, talks about them when they are fully formed • Makes fewer contacts but stays with them for longer • More interested in ideas than people
Extroverted learner	**Introverted learner**
• Learns by doing and experimenting with new approaches • Keen to put ideas into action – ideas are only useful when applied • Talks freely to others and happily disseminates knowledge and ideas	• Learns by reflecting and thinking and is more cautious about new approaches • Likes to understand an issue but less anxious to put it into practice • Talks to like-minded people but slower to disseminate knowledge

SUMMARY

You should by now have a good idea of your natural style – whether you prefer to approach networking from a business, relationships, ideas or learning perspective, and whether you do so as an extrovert or an introvert. This is the starting point for your networking campaign. You need to understand your most preferred approach but then you must also learn new ways to make connections with people and build those connections to positive working relationships. Both extroverts and introverts have their own challenges with networking but to be fully effective we need to learn a complete set of skills. Some of these skills will come naturally to you; others will need more application to develop. We examine these in the next part of *Powerful Networking*.

Part three

DEVELOPING THE SKILLS OF NETWORKING

Networking requires skill and practice. As we saw in part Two, some people are enthusiastic networkers and some are more reluctant. The enthusiasts are not necessarily better than the reluctant as there are a range of skills that networkers need to learn. As in most skill areas, effectiveness is a factor of both motivation and capability. Motivation alone is not enough because the outcome of networking depends on the skill and approach of the networker.

In this part of *Powerful Networking* we will look at eleven key skills for the networker. Each skill will be put into context and then described in terms of positive behaviours and negative. There will be a brief summary of how to develop these skills and any important techniques you can use.

The skills we will be examining are:

1 clarifying goals and objectives for networking

2 identifying networking opportunities

3 making the initial connections

4 building rapport with your contacts

5 developing positive long-term relationships within your network

6 influencing skills and positive politics

7 building visibility so that people approach you to join their network

8 reciprocity – the basis of effective networking relationships

9 extending and maintaining your
network

10 keeping track of your contacts by
effective record keeping

11 resilience in the face of fear and
opposition.

This list is not exhaustive but covers the key
skills that help networks grow and develop.
The skills are largely behavioural as networking requires good interpersonal skills – some
people are almost born with the skills and
some need to work hard to acquire them.
There is no doubt that effective networkers
understand people and their needs.

Research done by David Mayer and Herbert
M. Greenberg on 'What makes a good sales-
man', reported in the *Harvard Business Review*
in July/August 1964, was based on a hypothe-
sis that a good sales representative has two
basic qualities: empathy and ego drive. The
empathy helps to understand the other person's perspective; the ego drive gives you the
confidence to keep growing and developing
your network in pursuit of your career and
personal goals. Selling is a good analogy for
networking – you are selling your ideas, your
value as a contact and your trustworthiness as
a friend. But like all good sales people, you are
developing long-term relationships not short-
term 'deals'. The skills described through the
rest of this chapter show you how.

....

CLARIFYING GOALS AND OBJECTIVES FOR NETWORKING

You should have gained from the previous section a sense of the many benefits of networking. Networking is an important process in your development not just because it can introduce you to people who can help you in the growth of your career or your business, but also because you can meet people who can provide support, can introduce you to new ideas, provide coaching or just be good friends.

Within this broad range of activity, you do need to narrow down your networking priorities at any particular time to meet particular needs. We can't spend all our time networking, although most people I know would be more effective if they spent more time than they currently do. You have to identify the important priorities for your networking activities, depending on your goals and objectives elsewhere in your lives.

Why is clarifying goals and objectives important?

Clarifying your goals and objectives is important in two main areas:

- setting goals for your overall networking campaign
- clarifying specific objectives for particular networking meetings.

The difference between goals and objectives is quite simple. I use goals in the sense of broad aspirations and intentions, supported by objectives, the specific and measurable short-term actions that enable goals to be achieved. You will have some broad goals for carrying out your networking campaign, based on your particular needs in the present state of your career. These will need to be supported by setting clear objectives for each of your networking meetings.

This clarity of purpose doesn't mean that every meeting has to be scheduled and time-tabled like a military operation. It does mean that you should have a broad idea of the purpose of your networking activities and you should be working towards this purpose during your networking meetings. This clarity of purpose is important for a number of reasons:

- You have only a limited amount of time for networking and it is important to ensure that your time is well used. Networking without purpose can easily become pure socialising, which is very enjoyable but unlikely to make any real difference to your career or your business.

- Your networking priorities at any particular time will be based around your specific needs of the moment. Networking can have a powerful impact on those needs provided they are clearly stated.

- Networking involves interaction between at least two people. If you initiate a meeting without a clear set of objectives, you are wasting someone else's time as well as your own. With someone you don't know well, you may have only one chance to establish a good relationship and this will be badly damaged if they believe that you have no real purpose in meeting.

How do you set goals and objectives?

Goal setting for your networking campaign requires some clear goals for your career, your business or your current job. As we have already seen, networking is a process that can help you in a variety of ways – ideas genera-tion, personal development, business connec-tions or just stress reduction with your soul mates. At different times in your career, some elements will be more important than others and you need to make sure that you have a clear focus on those higher priorities.

✎ Think about these questions:

- What are your career goals? What are you trying to achieve?
- Where are your strengths and what are your weaknesses? Who do you know who can help you resolve some of your weaknesses?
- What particular issues are important in your career and your life right now?
- Where would you most benefit from developing new contacts? What people or types of people would be most helpful to you at the moment?
- Where do you need an injection of new ideas? Which businesses do you respect? How can you get to talk to them?

Each meeting or contact then requires a clear set of objectives. Before going in to meetings ask yourself:

- What do I want to get from this meeting? How does it further my goals?
- What will the other people want to get out of the meeting? How can I help them meet their goals and objectives?
- How long do I have or how long do I need?
- What do I need to know about my contact or their business? What basic research do I need to have done beforehand?
- How will I measure the success of the meeting?

How good are you at goal and objective setting?

Positive indicators for goal and objective setting

✎ Do you:

	YES	NO
have a clear set of career goals in place?	☐	☐
find that you have contacts that help you resolve most of your business problems?	☐	☐
have productive meetings with others and make progress after each discussion?	☐	☐

set yourself a clear objective for
most of your meetings and clarify
that with the other people in the
discussion?   ☐   ☐

find that people are contacting you
because you add so much value to
their work?   ☐   ☐

Negative indicators for goal and objective setting

✎ Do you:

	YES	NO
find that you are uncertain about your objectives for your career and your job?	☐	☐
find it difficult to identify people to help you or support your ideas?	☐	☐
get stuck with your work and find it difficult to move forward?	☐	☐
find it difficult to identify a clear objective for your meetings?	☐	☐
spend time in aimless networking and socialising without getting any particular business benefit?	☐	☐
find that people don't approach you for support for their projects?	☐	☐

If you feel that the negatives outweigh the
positive in your self-assessment, then you
need to develop a more goal-focused approach

to networking and to clarify your objectives for your networking meetings. This involves asking yourself the questions set out on page 94 before each meeting. It also involves understanding your own career goals and current work goals more effectively so that you have a clear idea where you need to focus your networking effort so that you can get more 'bang' for your networking 'buck'.

Tips for networking meetings

Some simple development tips are:

- Observe people who you feel have a clear focus when they go into meetings. How do they clarify objectives? And how do they keep the meeting on track without appearing brusque or rude?

- Like an athlete before a race, spend a little time visualising the outcome that you require from a meeting. Learn to see the positive benefits for all the parties of a successful outcome.

- Practise writing down a one- or two-sentence summary of what you want to get from each meeting. If it takes more than a couple of sentences then try again – you should be able to describe it succinctly to yourself, so that you can describe it concisely to your networking partner.

....

IDENTIFYING NETWORKING OPPORTUNITIES

An important feature of networking is the maintenance of a sharp alertness to networking opportunities. Effective networkers are on the alert for opportunities to grow and develop their range of contacts; less effective networkers will not recognise the importance of chance contacts or the possibilities available to them within their current network.

The clarity of goals combined with alertness for opportunities is a winning combination as it combines purpose with opportunism. Many business strategies are based on real clarity of purpose and yet others are based on speed of reaction to a change in the marketplace. In networking, we need to harness the power of both approaches.

This section will focus on three major skill areas:

- identifying opportunities within your current network
- identifying opportunities to build good relationships with people that you meet
- targeting individuals who you want to include in your network.

Why are these skills important?

These networking skills are important because:

- they create a sense of alertness to opportunities that will be particularly useful to you as your career progresses

- they will give a sense of purpose to your relationship building and make you identify what you can gain from particular relationships ... and what you can contribute
- they will help you to become proactive in identifying and contacting people who you want to meet as well as maintaining your existing set of contacts.

Identifying opportunities within your current network

You will have already identified a network of people with whom you work well and who fit into the categories set out in part One of *Powerful Networking*. Those are people who can fulfil a particular need for you in a specific area of your life and work. These are probably people with whom you already have a good relationship and you have probably developed this relationship informally and without any particular purpose. Your task in this part of your networking campaign is to identify ways in which you can extend the relationship into other areas of mutual benefit.

You can do this quite painlessly without appearing to be too pushy or to be 'using' the other person. If you extend the relationship effectively, you will both benefit and, as we shall see later in this chapter, the exploration of issues for mutual benefit is an important part of building enduring relationships based on successful collaboration.

✎ Look at your current network and ask yourself:

- How can these people help me achieve my career objectives or to do a better job at work?
- How can I help them to achieve their objectives more effectively?
- Who are the really high octane networkers in my circle of contacts and how can they help me to extend my network?

An important factor in making the most use of your existing network is to make them more aware of your goals and aspirations and to be prepared to open up discussions with them more quickly. As we shall see later, effective networking relationships go beyond socialising into a deeper understanding of both parties' aspirations and personal objectives.

Identifying opportunities to build good relationships with new contacts

Meeting new people is obviously a key part of networking. Effective networkers, however, see the possibilities for new contacts to introduce them to new ideas or to make other new contacts. They are able to explain their agenda quickly to others and this stimulates discussion about the possibilities for a mutually beneficial networking relationship.

When you meet someone for the first time:

- try to understand their background and experience as quickly as possible
- explain your own experience and aspirations when you spot an appropriate opportunity to do so

- ask how you can help them and try to identify ways that they can help you.

The most productive approach is to maintain an alertness to opportunities to move beyond a brief social or business encounter towards a more productive networking relationship. We look at the skills of building rapport and extending the relationship later.

Targeting people who you think can help you

What if you need a network partner who isn't currently in your web of contacts? There are many reasons why this might occur:

- Your business may be going through major restructuring and you need to talk to someone in a different business who has gone through a similar experience.

- You may be looking to expand your business into a different area and you need to find contacts who may be looking for a joint venture.

- You may be a consultant who wants to build a client list in a new industry.

- You may be considering a career change and you want to talk to an expert in your new field.

In these situations you will probably need to deliberately expand your network to include people who have the experience that you want to tap. There are several ways of doing this:

- Make a point of consulting your own network to find out people who may have that experience or who may know other people who have it. If you have good relationships with people you will be able to ask them directly: 'Who do you know who works in financial services?', 'Who would you talk to about mergers and acquisitions?'

- Identify a business or an organisation that is particularly good at what you want to do or to know. Then identify the relevant person within that organisation and approach them directly. But make sure that you have clarified your purpose in approaching them beforehand and have identified what support you may be able to offer in return.

- Target well-known people within a profession or industry, who you feel may be able to provide you with help or support. Research their backgrounds and try to understand the important aspects of their work before you make contact with them. Asking them questions which are already in the public domain is a waste of both their time and yours – and gives a poor first impression of someone who has not done their homework well.

- Think through a strategy to enable you to make contact with them:
  - Do you have contacts in common?
  - Do you belong to the same institutes or professional bodies?
  - Do you have similar hobbies or interests?
  - How might you meet them and how should you make the first approach?

How good are you at identifying network opportunities?

Positive indicators for identifying opportunities

✎ Do you:

	YES	NO
have a good knowledge of your contacts – their aims, aspirations and the contacts of their networks?	☐	☐
have a good understanding of the key organisations and influential individuals in your industry and profession?	☐	☐
keep alert to opportunities to explain your goals and aspirations to other people? Are you alert to their interests and personal objectives?	☐	☐
find meeting people and exchanging views and ideas easy?	☐	☐

Negative indicators for identifying opportunities

✎ Do you:

	YES	NO
find it difficult to explain the wider interests of your current network?	☐	☐
feel embarrassed to ask for other contacts from your network partners?	☐	☐
feel unable to identify role models or benchmark organisations within your industry or profession?	☐	☐
find meeting new people a difficult experience and feel that you don't establish a good relationship quickly?	☐	☐

If the negatives outweigh the positives you can develop a sharper alertness to opportunities by clarifying your own objectives and tuning in to the needs and objectives of others. Talk to people who seem to be highly socially skilled and who have a wide network and try to work out how they identify opportunities without embarrassment. The remainder of this section should help you develop some skills to help overcome any embarrassment that you may have in asking for support and help.

....

MAKING THE INITIAL CONNECTIONS

After the planning and the objective setting, the first real networking activity is the first connection. This is the most critical and yet the most difficult move. Mistakes made at this stage can at worst stop the relationship in its tracks and at best give the wrong impression which may take some time to undo.

The way you make connections with others sets the tone for the rest of your dealings with them in the future. If you are too timid or vague, they will think that you have little of interest to say. If they see you as too pushy, they will feel that they will always be fending you away.

You need to plan your first contact very carefully because it is the most difficult and because you will probably feel particularly unsure of how to approach the first meeting. When we are most unsure of ourselves, we need to plan more carefully to ensure that the first discussions at least go well.

Options for the first contact

GOLDEN RULE 6

Find ways to make connections with people for your networks quickly.

There are four main ways to make contact with someone you don't know:

- by telephone

- by letter or other mailshot
- by electronic mail
- face to face.

The advantages and disadvantages of each have been well covered in other communications programmes, but the following notes may help to clarify when you should use each medium and how it should be used effectively.

Contact by telephone

The telephone is an informal medium and is very accessible. You can make a telephone call quickly and without the need to script your messages as carefully as you would a letter. It can be useful for making exploratory noises to people and allows you to get rapid feedback on the enthusiasm of the other party for the development of a long-term relationship.

Positive features	**Negative features**
• Informality – the telephone is an informal way of getting to know someone quickly	• Preparation – it is difficult to anticipate the direction of the discussion and to prepare for every eventuality
• Feedback – the telephone enables immediate interaction and can move an initial contact on very quickly	• Mood – you can't predict the mood of the person you are calling, nor can you be sure that you are calling at the right time
• Transience – proposals made over the telephone can be rephrased and repositioned	• Courage – cold calling requires a large amount of courage and many people find it difficult to work up the courage to make an unannounced telephone call

Positive features	**Negative features**
• Simplicity – all you need to know is a name and a telephone number	• Barriers – many senior people don't answer their own telephones and you may need to persuade someone else to give you access to your 'target'
• Rapport – you can build rapport quicker by tuning in to the receiver's comments and ideas	• Easy exit – either party can end the conversation at any time without the consent of the other party

The telephone is a good medium for people you already know or with whom you have a strong connection. Otherwise, it is a difficult medium on its own. You can improve your effectiveness on the telephone by:

- clarifying your reason for calling and rehearsing two or three opening phrases that summarise your objectives. This enables you to overcome the initial nervousness of a cold approach

- always asking 'Is this a good time to talk?' after introducing yourself. If it isn't then ask 'When would be a convenient time for us to talk?' Then stick to that time. If you are talking to a secretary or PA, try to find out when would be a good time to talk to your contact. Try to find out a little about their routine, so that you are avoiding a discussion at a time when they have competing priorities

- anticipating some likely objections – but remember, you are trying to build a good working relationship, not selling double glazing, and so you shouldn't try to overcome objections but rather you should try to understand them. The aim of a telephone call is not to build a relationship but to arrange a meeting – which is the most effective way of building enduring relationships.

Contact by letter

The letter is a colder and more formal medium. It is usually more considered and as it is a one-way communication it enables you to state your case without any interruption from the other party. It allows for no initial interaction but can act as a good introduction.

Positive features

- Clarity – you can prepare your letter, check it over and recheck it for possible confusion, before mailing it

- Information – you can transmit a lot of information through the mail

- Timing – a letter is less intrusive than other media; it can be read at the convenience of the receiver (and it requires less courage to send)

- Image – a well-constructed letter on a well-designed letterhead acts as a permanent reminder of your message

Negative features

- Feedback – you get little immediate feedback from the recipient so you can't adjust the tone of your letter if you have somehow missed the mark

- Information – you may include unnecessary or irrelevant information through not knowing the needs of the receiver

- Timing – you can't guarantee the mood of the recipient when they receive the letter, or that the right person has read it

- Persuasion – unless you are a brilliant copyriter, it is unlikely that a letter alone will be persuasive

Positive features	**Negative features**
• Transferability – a letter can be passed on to a more appropriate recipient if your original contact is not quite the right person	• The WPB – a letter is a fragile thing that can be screwed up and thrown in the Waste Paper Bin

The letter alone is not a persuasive medium but it can make an effective introduction and it requires less courage for those of us who dread the prospect of a cold call. The objective of a letter is to make an appointment for a meeting and so it needs to be brief and concise, explaining in no more than three brief paragraphs why you want to meet up, what your objectives are and a sense of how a meeting might be helpful to your contact.

End your letter by saying how you intend to follow up the initial contact and then make sure you do that when you have said you will. Enclosing a brief CV can be helpful, or a business brochure if you have one. They give more information about you and should help the recipient to identify why you would make a good addition to their network. They should be well produced and not untidy or out of date. The style and format of the letter will say more about you than the content.

Contact by e-mail

Electronic mail is an important networking medium as it combines the advantages of written communication with the immediacy and accessibility of the telephone. E-mail gives you access straight to an individual and can encourage an immediate response; you can also spend a little time preparing your message and can take time in framing your response to the other person.

I personally find e-mail to be an excellent networking device, particularly as you can reply promptly to an e-mail as the system almost begs you to send a response to each message received. They are a powerful internal communication process within an organisation, although they are no substitute for face-to-face interaction.

Positive features

- Accessibility – providing you have an e-mail address you can make direct contact; the e-mail stays in the In Tray until answered and it can be transferred to a more appropriate person automatically. E-mails are no more complex to send across the globe than across the street

- Preparation – you can take time to prepare your e-mail and to make any subsequent responses

- Brevity – you can make an e-mail as short or as long as you wish. The cost of e-mails is very low and you can send out multiple e-mails at a fraction of the cost of 'snail mail'

Negative features

- Permanence – e-mails can be deleted at a touch of a button and your carefully crafted note can be consigned to cyberspace

- Impersonality – your e-mail is not normally relayed in a personal way and has very little on it to distinguish you from other writers (e.g. no letter headings, signatures or colour brochures). The only differentiator is the content

- Access – some people ask their secretaries or PAs to answer their e-mail and they have the power of deletion or providing a stock response

Positive features	Negative features
• Information – you can attach a file or files of information without depleting a forest	• Technophobia – some senior people are not yet sufficiently IT literate to work their e-mail. The young use it all the time
• Intrusion – the e-mail is not as intrusive as a telephone call; it will be answered when the recipient checks their e-mail	• Relationship building – you can't build a good relationship on e-mail alone, although there are news stories about cyber romances!

E-mail will become the key mechanism for making initial contacts and keeping in touch. You can't build an enduring relationshp via e-mail but you can keep in touch much more easily and efficiently (and cheaply) than with other forms of remote communication. It ends the awful game of telephone tag and of letters being lost in the post. If you are serious about networking then you must be on e-mail. Aside from e-mail, the other benefit of connection to the Internet, particularly accessing the World Wide Web (WWW), is that it is a great source of ideas and contacts.

The WWW is a collection of sites, designed with a single computer language containing hyperlinks which enable each site to be linked together in the form of a network. You can develop your own site, or home page, and access other people's home pages very simply by either using their Web site address (usually prefixed by http://www.) or by clicking on highlighted text and moving from site to site.

This is not the place to give you a detailed review of the Internet, except for its implications for networking. The WWW will become an increasingly important source of contacts and ideas in the future. You may wish to set up your own home page so that people can contact you more easily. There are a number of books on selling and marketing on the Internet which will help you set one up.

In the future, more and more businesses will recruit through the Internet and the era of the electronic CV is already upon us. Application forms are filled in through Web sites and recruitment literature viewed on the Web rather than sent to your home address. The Internet is not the only medium for networking, but it is and will become an important feature, enabling you to increase your access to ideas and contacts, particularly to make that initial contact.

Making contact face to face

There are many opportunities to make contact face to face with people. These first contacts happen either purposely or spontaneously. You may have been given a contact and decided to meet them at a conference or at another event which you know they will attend, or you will meet someone by chance and identify that you both have some interests in common and arrange to meet again.

Face-to-face meetings are not often the first contact but are the result of an exchange of letters or e-mails or a telephone conversation. The old sales rep trick of camping out in a potential contact's office is almost always counterproductive (although it gives you high marks for persistence).

The first face-to-face contact after an exchange of letters is an important meeting. You will have identified some interests in common and may have struck up some kind of relationship over the telephone. You should have done some research about your contact but you will not know them as a person – their approach, style and manner. The next section looks at the development of rapport with new contacts but we still need to look at some options for arranging the first meeting.

The meeting can take place at your office, at their office, over a meal or at a neutral meeting place. Lunch is a popular networking tool (or dinner or breakfast) but it is a high risk option with someone you don't know. It may be a great success and the informal atmosphere may work particularly well, but there are so many variables – the venue, the food, the drink, the service, the ambience and the bill – that it becomes a difficult meeting to manage. Networking over drinks or meals should probably be left until you know someone well enough to predict their tastes and reduce the tension in the event.

Meetings at their office creates less effort for them as you are doing the travelling and fitting around their comfort zones rather than expecting them to fit around yours. An office environment is easier to control – it is geared to business and not to entertaining. Either it is your own office so you can manage the details such as seating arrangements, coffee and an uninterrupted environment, or it will be in your contact's office, so you can respond to their lead, knowing that their arrangements will at least be making them more comfortable.

If there are difficult issues around the dynamics of meeting in an office, then a neutral meeting place can be helpful. Hotels with large foyers and coffee areas are a good neutral venue, as are institutions with large meeting areas in the centre of large cities. For example, I use the Directors' Room in the Institute of Directors in Pall Mall as a meeting venue. It is ideal – in the centre of London, a spacious room with waiter service for tea, coffee and sandwiches available. If you are meeting in an external venue, arrive early and check it beforehand to ensure you know the layout and any other arrangements you need to know – e.g. the procedure for ordering coffee, the location of the toilets and some of the other minor issues that take the tension out of the first meeting.

Chance face-to-face meetings, on the other hand, can be very powerful because of their spontaneity. You may meet at a conference, an institute meeting or a social event. Conferences are particularly good places to meet new contacts as they are normally held by a group of people with a common interest – a shared profession (e.g. human resources or finance), industry (e.g. retailing or banking) or common interest (e.g. quality) or membership of a common group (alumni of a particular business school). This means that you have a strong chance of meeting people who share common interests and so the initial problems of identifying those common interests are overcome.

Rules for networking at conferences

However, some people can come away from a conference with many contacts and others leave without a solitary business card. The essential difference is back to the two features of the good sales person – empathy and ego drive. Empathy gives you a real interest in other people's ideas and background, ego drive gives you the confidence to approach people and get to know them better. A few simple rules for effective networking at conferences are:

- Get hold and keep hold of the list of attendees; mark those people who you would like to meet and look out for them.

- Make sure you wear any name badge you are given and introduce yourself clearly to other delegates.

- Remember the names of people you meet at conferences and write them down for future reference.

- Participate fully in the conference, asking questions of the speakers where possible (always state your name and your organisation) and offer to make syndicate presentations if these are required.

- Use tea and coffee breaks to meet new people, particularly those you have 'targeted' to meet.

- Write to any attendees or speakers with whom you want to keep in contact. A brief congratulatory letter is a good introduction, saying how much you enjoyed their contribution, and a possible request for a meeting, suggesting how a meeting with you will help them as well.

- Let the conference organisers know if you are prepared to speak at future events – better still, join the organising committee; this puts you in a gatekeeper role for the conference and gives you the opportunity to meet several industry or professional experts in the search for conference speakers.

How good are you at making the first connection?

Positive indicators of good contact making

✎ Do you:

	YES	NO
emerge from meetings and conferences with a range of new contacts and new ideas?	☐	☐
have a positive approach to the telephone, writing business letters and e-mailing?	☐	☐
introduce yourself clearly and without embarrassment?	☐	☐
follow up initial contacts with a letter or telephone call?	☐	☐

Negative indicators of making contacts

✎ Do you:

	YES	NO
leave events without making a single contact?	☐	☐

avoid making telephone calls or
writing to people you wish to
contact?   ☐   ☐

feel nervous or hesitant when
meeting new people?   ☐   ☐

let contacts drop very quickly and
forget names easily?   ☐   ☐

If your negative responses outweigh your
positive, develop an approach to making contacts that eases the pain for you. Draft an introductory letter and ensure that you are very happy with it before sending it out. Script the first few phrases of your telephone calls and write a note reminding yourself of the things you want to achieve in the call. Practise introducing yourself with a couple of confident phrases and visualise introducing yourself to others.

If you aren't naturally good at making contacts or introductions, rehearse until you are. The most difficult part of networking is the initial introduction. If you can overcome that hurdle then you will really start to enjoy the process and gain much more from it. Don't depend on one approach. You will find a number of ways to make initial contact – for many people, a letter, followed by a telephone call and then a meeting is the best combination; others may find a different approach is better for them. Find an approach that is right for you and right for the situation.

| **GOLDEN RULE 7** |

Use different media to keep in touch with your network.

BUILDING RAPPORT WITH CONTACTS

The objective of networking, or at least of really powerful networking, is to build enduring relationships based on mutual friendship and reciprocity. Some of your initial contacts will remain just that – contacts. Others will grow into productive relationships and some will even become lasting friendships. The reason why some relationships grow and some don't is the degree of rapport between the two parties.

Think back to your school or university. Some people you have forgotten, some you can remember but have not kept in contact with, others are still contacts, but some may have become lifelong friends. In the business world, the same hierarchy of relationships applies – contacts, colleagues, friends, soul mates – all based to some degree or other on the level of rapport. Rapport comes naturally in some relationships and requires more careful nurturing in others. It is something that some people find easy and natural, while others are more private people and feel they have to work at it.

Tips on tuning in

GOLDEN RULE 8

Try to get on people's wavelengths as quickly as possible.

Building rapport is like tuning your receiver on to the same wavelength as someone else's transmitter. It is a must if the discussions are to be fully effective. There are some things that you can do to build rapport more effectively with other people:

- Listen carefully to their point of view and try to understand it effectively. Stephen Covey in his book *The Seven Habits of Highly Effective People* suggests that people should 'seek first to understand and then be understood'. While you must have a view of your own objectives before you go into a meeting, your primary purpose if you are to develop an effective working relationship is to understand the other person, their perspectives and motivations.

- Listen carefully to the words and phrases they use and the way they express themselves. You can then use similar words and phrases when you describe your interests and motivations. Practitioners of NLP (neuro linguistic programming) believe strongly that effective communication stems from rapport and rapport comes from seeing and describing the world from the perspective of the other person. If that other person uses visual words ('I see that ... ', 'My vision for this project is ... ') then it will be helpful if you use visual words and, figuratively, paint a picture for them.

- Ask questions to understand their perspective more effectively. Ask open questions and be prepared to probe their responses – not to catch them out but to understand them better. If you develop a good questioning technique, you can help them understand their approach much better because you are approaching the subject in a different way and really getting into the important issues.

- Be open yourself. You can't expect people to open up to you if you are cagey and reticent. Part of your initial assessment of the individual involves making an assessment of how open they are being with you and how open you can be with them. You should certainly match their level of openness but be a little circumspect about going too far until you are more sure about the relationship. Your degree of openness is a difficult judgement with someone you don't know well. Opening up too soon may leave you a little vulnerable but opening up too late may put the brakes on a potentially fruitful relationship.

GOLDEN RULE 9

Be open about your own goals and aspirations.

Why is rapport important?

Rapport is the force that deepens a relationship from transactional to transformational. Transactional relationships are based on an exchange of information but are at a relatively superficial level; transformational relationships make a real difference to our lives and provide us with real support and a genuinely fresh perspective to our lives.

Look at your network and work out which of your relationships are transactional and which are transformational.

✎ Answer these questions:

- What factors are significant in your deeper relationships that are absent in your transactional relationships?
- Which of your transactional relationships would you like to deepen?
- How might you do that?

How good are you at building rapport?

Positive indicators for rapport building

✎ Do you:

	YES	NO
sense real progress in your networking meetings with colleagues?	☐	☐
feel confident enough to be open about your goals and aspirations with other people?	☐	☐
have discussions on deeper issues – both your issues and theirs?	☐	☐

discuss with other people their own
problems and help them open up
about their concerns? ☐ ☐

feel able to give your contacts
feedback and to challenge them on
important issues? ☐ ☐

Negative indicators for rapport building

✎ Do you:

	YES	NO
base most of your relationships on an exchange of information and little more?	☐	☐
feel that your meetings are constrained by some invisible force?	☐	☐
base most of your discussions on technical and professional issues rather than personal issues?	☐	☐
know little about your work contacts' personal or family lives?	☐	☐
deal more in facts than in values?	☐	☐
feel unsure of how your colleagues feel about important issues?	☐	☐

A preponderance of answers around the negative indicators suggests that you may need to work harder at developing rapport with your networking partners. Some networkers have a large wad of business cards but few really deep networking relationships; others make fewer contacts but they lead to deeper and more productive relationships. The aim is to move your relationships from a superficial/transactional level to a deeper and more transformational level, so that they make a difference to your life and your network partners.

Developing empathy

GOLDEN RULE 10

Understand other people's goals and interests before focusing on your own.

Rapport building is based on empathy. Without genuine empathy rapport building is a slick technique. It was once flippantly said about sincerity that 'once you could fake that, you could fake anything'. Many people believe the same about empathy, believing that it is a set of techniques that help you manipulate people and bring them round to your way of thinking. The least empathetic person I have ever worked with regularly asked people 'How do you feel?', and thought that this was empathy in action.

Empathy is rooted in a strong desire to see things from the other person's perspective. It is the basis of good working relationships based on mutual trust and understanding and is not a superficial technique for persuading or manipulating others. Some of the following points should help to develop a greater understanding of yourself and your approach to people as well as developing your own capacity for understanding and valuing the needs and values of others:

- Make a list of your major prejudices – personality types, behaviours, topics on which you have strong opinions – these will be the barriers to your thinking. Make a conscious effort to control these prejudices when you meet them at work.

- Get feedback from colleagues when you have had a discussion with them – ask if you gave them enough airspace.

- Practise reflecting back feelings to people.

- Become a people watcher – enjoy interpreting their body language and their tone of voice. In meetings, watch people carefully and try to identify what they are feeling and anticipate their approach during the next discussion.

- Develop a good working relationship with someone you don't like or someone who has a different approach to life and work.

- Learn to take your own emotional temperature – monitor your own responses and feelings regularly, particularly on contentious issues.

- Take a complex issue you are dealing with now – one that involves some complex 'political' issues. Write down a list of the parties involved; describe their issues and motives; plan how you will address the issue while respecting their values.

- Reflect on an issue where you failed to gain commitment – what were the key interpersonal issues and how did you tackle them? How could that have been improved?

✎ Answer the following questions. They may help you to focus on the development of empathy from your perspective:

- Where do you 'lose the plot'? Where do your prejudices stop you listening effectively to others?
- How does your personal style impact on other people – do you dominate or hold back?
- How comfortable are you in discussions about people's feelings?
- How well do you know how people feel about particular issues? How much is hidden and how much is visible with careful observation?
- What type of people do you relate well to? What types do you find more difficult? Why?
- What are the key issues that you are facing? What are your beliefs and values in relation to this issue? What are the beliefs, values and motives of others?
- How well do you think through other people's responses to issues? What method do you have for ensuring that you do this?
- Where do you face the most opposition? How well do you understand why?
- How do you get feedback about your style and approach?

DEVELOPING POSITIVE LONG-TERM RELATIONSHIPS

The move from connections and rapport into a long-term relationship is what makes networking so satisfying. Some networkers have many, many superficial relationships and tick them off one by one, keeping in touch but probably never gaining the real benefit from the relationship.

The relationships in our lives that we most value are those that move to a deeper level of intimacy, when we go beyond mutual back-scratching towards a deeper understanding of each other's needs and values. These relationships may not always be based on an agreement of each other's approach to life and may often be with people who are very different from us, but there are some important elements of effective working relationships that we need to understand if we are to take our networking beyond superficiality.

Why is it important to develop effective long-term relationships?

People are complex and multifaceted. What you see with many people is most certainly not all that you get. It takes time and patience to understand people's values and to learn much from them. It is said that to know a city or country, you should either visit for a day or a lifetime – a day visit will give you a vivid first impression, a lifetime will enable you to know the interesting and subtle features which underpin that first impression. It is the same with people – the first impression is important but it takes a lifetime to really understand and value the subtle nuances that go to make up a complex individual.

Most people take some time to open up and talk freely about their thoughts and ideas. Moving from superficiality to greater depth in a relationship requires trust that confidences won't be damaged and a greater appreciation of the mutual benefit to be gained from the relationship.

Strong positive relationships lead to other relationships. People will only introduce others whom they trust into their own personal network. We don't make connection between other people when we feel that they may damage our own personal relationships.

Deeper relationships are more interesting and more fun than superficial contacts. They require less work at the beginning of each meeting as rapport is already in place and so each contact is more quickly effective and productive.

The building blocks of good long-term relationships

There are many books on the market about developing long-term relationships and this section is not intended to give an in-depth review of relationship building, but rather to point to some of the important components of good working relationships so that you can analyse some of your own relationships and identify how they can be deepened for mutual benefit.

Not all of your relationships will deepen and

develop and you shouldn't be concerned if they don't all meet these criteria. You should certainly be concerned if none of them do! I have picked on the following six building blocks that form the basis of positive relationships – they are neither exclusive nor exhaustive, but they form a good basis for your own thinking in this area.

Understanding

We have already looked at the basis of rapport and empathy. Neither of these ideas are rooted in agreement or similarity, but are based on a motivation and capability to understand each other's perspective. Relationships must be based on mutual understanding and that understanding should deepen as the relationship develops. Unless you have a good idea of how others see the world and what their interests are, you are unlikely to develop an effective working relationship with them.

GOLDEN RULE 11

Build long-term relationships based on mutual understanding.

Communication

Understanding requires good communication. You can't understand other people, or they you, without clear communication. Good communications should be positive and open, for the more openly you communicate the less basis there is for suspicion and the faster the growth of trust. The more we know of other people's ideas and thoughts and the more

they know of ours, the more deeply we
understand and appreciate them and their
value as a colleague and friend. Every relationship, formal or informal, individual or collective, deepens when the level of communication increases. The last political act before a
declaration of war is the severing of diplo-
matic ties – the breaking of the lines of
communications.

| GOLDEN RULE 12 |

Become an interesting conversationalist.

Reliability

Communication falters when either party is
felt not to be communicating accurately or
consistently. The understanding we gain
through communication is useless if on subsequent meetings the other party has substan-
tially changed their approach or values. Reli-
ability is an important basis for a relationship
as it moves on from the ephemeral to the
substantial. When we feel we can rely on
someone the relationship becomes based on
mutual obligations and the bonds that tie the
two parties together become stronger. If we
feel the relationship is based on a fleeting
notion of personal interests, we are less prepared to invest time in building it.

Mutual acceptance

Agreement and congruence of views are not
the most important part of a relationship.
Many of the most productive working relationships are based on extreme differences of

style, temperament and approach. The philosophy underpinning psychometric questionnaires like Belbin's Team Role and the Myers–Briggs Type Inventory is to celebrate the positive benefits of working with people who are different from us. The important principle is to value that difference and to see the value of an alternative perspective. Mutual acceptance of a different way of working and thinking is one of the most important issues for a relationship; it enables the relationship to grow and the two parties to develop in their own way without damaging its base. Learn to accept people who have different views and value the freshness of perspective they bring rather than focusing exclusively on people who are like you and who think like you.

Splitting process from content

See the relationship as a process rather than just focusing on the substance or content of your discussions. Work hard to manage the relationship and try to identify ways to deepen it and make it more productive for both parties. One of the reasons for the breakdown of a relationship is when one or both parties have ceased to see their relationship as a separate entity and have stopped paying attention to it and nurturing it.

Mutual gain

Balance is an important condition of a relationship. For a relationship to be fruitful and productive both parties need to feel that they are gaining from it. Once a relationship becomes a one-way street it loses balance and the party that is losing the most will begin to disengage. Both parties should be thinking not just of their own interests but of how they can support the other person in the fulfilment of their objectives.

This is particularly important if there is a disagreement in a relationship. The best relationships are those where each party is looking for solutions that create mutual benefit. Employee relations are always more effective when instead of trying to damage the other party, the focus is on both sides helping and supporting each other to meet their goals. While both parties are gaining something useful from their relationship, it will grow and develop. When it becomes unbalanced, a relationship ultimately withers and dies.

How good are you at building long-term relationships?

Positive indicators of building positive long-term relationships

---

✎ Do you:

	YES	NO
find many of your relationships grow and develop into closer working relationships or friendships?	☐	☐
find many of your contacts keep in touch with you to ask for help and advice?	☐	☐
feel able to describe the positive attributes that you gain from each of your relationships?	☐	☐

Negative indicators of building positive long-term relationships

---

✎ Do you:

	YES	NO
find many of your relationships remain as just contacts?	☐	☐
initiate all your contacts rather than other people contacting you for help and advice?	☐	☐
'use' your relationships for your own benefit rather than considering them as being mutually beneficial?	☐	☐
feel that the other party gains more than you do?	☐	☐

If the negatives outweigh the positives you should pay more attention to converting your contacts from superficial members of your network to real network partners with whom you can enter into a much more fulfilling and fruitful relationship. You can do this by being more open about your goals and aspirations and by finding out more from your contacts to identify how they feel that you can develop a more positive partnership.

Not all of your relationships will grow and develop, but some of them should if both parties are to gain more from them. Networking is a lifetime process, not a short-term activity to meet a specific immediate need, and it is both healthy and desirable that some of your networking contacts should grow into deeper and more productive relationships.

....

INFLUENCING SKILLS AND POSITIVE POLITICS

Influencing and political skills are an important part of networking, particularly within your own organisation where increasing your level of influence over key decisions is an important feature of your career development. Many senior executives are derailed and sidelined because of their inability to perform effectively within the political environment that prevails within their organisation. Political skills are seen as a negative force by many people, particularly by those that don't possess them, and yet most effective executives are skilled in the political arts of influencing and lobbying.

Politics and influencing are combined in this section because they amount to almost the same thing. In the modern organisation, power is very widely dispersed, with less emphasis on a centralised bureaucracy and more on a network of functional and business specialists working together to achieve organisational goals. Many more decisions are made through making connections between people and functions and change comes about through gaining the support and commitment of others to a course of action – this requires good influencing skills and the ability to become an effective political operator.

The skills of the politician are useful to the networker. The politician sets policy goals, seeks the support of key people and bargains and negotiates to enable those objectives to be met. Holding a position of authority is no longer enough to be influential within an organisation. Authority has to be accompanied by a set of skills that enable that authority to be translated into practical action by knowing the right ways to do things and being able to enlist the support and commitment of key people.

Why influencing and political skills are important

Influencing and political skills are important because:

- they enable you to get things done within your organisation
- in a world with competing priorities they help you to ensure that your ideas and projects stay on the corporate agenda
- they help you gain the commitment and support of others for your personal agenda
- they keep you in the mainstream of your organisation and increase your awareness of what is going on and other people's future plans.

Politics isn't a devious exercise in getting your own way. It involves getting things done in an organisational setting and gaining the support and commitment of others. There are some simple influencing strategies that any professional in a modern organisation needs to understand – these strategies are useful whether you are developing a management development strategy in a major business, focusing on change in a professional institute or wanting to improve the workings of your school governors' meetings. These can be reduced down to six generic strategies:

- understand the strategy and culture of your organisation
- identify the power networks and the key stakeholders
- understand their style and objectives
- clarify the source of your own authority within the organisation
- clarify your own goals and work on your own agenda
- learn to make deals and negotiate.

Understand the strategy and culture of your organisation

You must know your organisation well if you are to become influential within it. The first task in your induction programme is to understand the main strategic priorities of the organisation and its cultural norms. Whatever your own agenda, you must work from a clear knowledge of the business imperatives and the behaviours and values that are most respected. There may be several subcultures within your organisation and you will need to understand them all. The key things you should know about your organisation are:

- the purpose and mission of the organisation
- the main strategic priorities and the current goals
- the values of the organisation – either explicit or implicit
- the key skills that are valued and respected

- the way things are changed and progressed
- behavioural norms.

Effective influencing within most organisations comes from first building rapport and credibility with the organisation. Even if your own agenda ultimately involves challenging the values and strategies of the organisation, you must first understand and respect them.

Identify the power networks and the key stakeholders

Every organisation has two sets of structure – the formal authority structure of budgets, systems and policy making and the informal structure of networks, norms and brokering deals. You need to know the formal authority structure to get new ideas signed off, but you need to be skilled at working the informal structure to get things done.

Think of most political systems in liberal democracies or even authoritarian regimes. They consist of a formal constitution and a complex set of procedures to ensure that the balance of power is maintained. Underneath the constitution is a mass of informal political activity – lobbying, making deals, gaining votes and seeking support for legislators' own ideas and interests. The constitution is the overarching framework in which these political activities are carried out and is there to ensure that change isn't too radical and that all legislation is consistently applied.

Within your own organisation try to work out where power lies and who, for each issue, are the real stakeholders. Stakeholders are the people who have a real interest in the out-come of an issue – they may be potential supporters or potential blocks depending on their perception of their own interests. You must also calculate the power that each of these groupings has within the organisation. Powerful supporters are great advocates for your ideas; powerful blocks can slow your progress up considerably. Your political strategies must take both groups into account. Your list of stakeholders should include the following:

- Your line manager – you will gain little support without taking your boss's views into account, although you need to understand their credibility within the organisation.

- Your 'functional' boss – if you work in a functional or specialist area then you will need to understand the views of your head of function.

- Your team and colleagues – your colleagues can damage your credibility if they don't support your views. Also, your direct reports need to be on-side and supportive of your ideas.

- Key line managers and senior executives within your organisation. You will need to identify the supporters and blocks in the formal structure.

- Key influencers in the informal structure – the people who, whatever their position, are listened to and their views respected. The important group to understand is the 'party of the future'. Identifying the people who have a clear picture of the organisation's future and are likely to be influential in getting there.

Understand their style and objectives

An important part of your influencing agenda is to understand the goals and objectives of your key stakeholders. You must know what they are trying to achieve and how they are trying to achieve it. There is a flow that takes place in organisations where ideas and proposals work well if they are consistent with the goals and objectives of key people. If they are moving against that flow then they are less likely to work. The flow stems from the changes in the industry, the organisation and its structures.

If the flow is towards giving more power to individual business units, then you will receive little support for a proposal that involves a large centralised team, taking power away from those units. You may however, gain support for an informal process that involves sharing best practice between the business units on an informal basis.

You also need to be aware of the style and approach of your key stakeholders. You must first build a good working relationship based on building effective rapport. If you work within individual comfort zones, then you will find an approach that is less likely to be blocked. I have seen many good proposals blocked because they have been too far outside someone's comfort zones. Different people require different approaches – some enjoy grappling with really radical ideas and others prefer incremental change. Try to understand the approach which fits each of your stake-holders.

Clarify the source of your own authority within the organisation

After understanding other people and their goals and norms, you need to understand yourself. Where does your authority come from? For people to achieve anything in an organisation they need to understand the source of their own authority. Power and authority stem from different sources. We each have a different profile depending on our position in the organisation or our background and experience. Some sources of authority are as follows.

Position power

The formal authority that relates to our role in the organisation and the levels of authority that stem from that. Position power leads to our authority to coerce, reward or instruct people to operate in a particular way. Position power involves using the legitimate authority that is inherent in our job or position. It can be used positively to encourage or support people or it can be used negatively to stop people behaving or performing in a particular way. It is usually more effective with 'subordinates', where you have the power to define and reward high performance or punish people for inappropriate behaviour. It is rarely enough to make a real difference within an organisation, unless you are the chairman or chief executive. Even at the highest level, the exclusive use of position power results in compliance and not commitment.

Expertise

Your knowledge base is an important factor in your level of influence. If you have a demonstrably high level of expertise, you will have a greater level of authority within the boundaries of your skill and knowledge. If you know more about corporate finance, employee legislation or gynaecology than most people in your organisation then your expert power will be higher, provided that you are able to use that expertise effectively and that you are seen as a credible person in other respects. If your knowledge base is an important source of power, then you should ensure that you keep it up to date, otherwise it will lose currency very quickly.

Personal power

There are some people who have qualities of energy, persuasiveness and personal impact and who find it easy to convince others to follow or avoid a particular policy. They are naturally influential and find it easy to state their case and to get their way. This is a necessary but not sufficient basis for an influencing strategy. Good presentation and communication skills are an important adjunct to other sources of power and authority but are not sufficient to make a real impact in an organisation.

Network power

The quality and extent of your personal network is an important factor in your power and influence in an organisation. The most influential people in an organisation are the 'gatekeepers' – the people who control the access to important networks. Often, network power is not aligned with position power and people in

relatively lowly positions can have dispropor-
tionate power because of the level and quality
of their contacts.

Moral authority

The highest degree of power and authority
stems from trust and respect. If people believe
in your credibility and your motives, then
your other sources of power will work much
more effectively for you. The type of politician
whom nobody likes or respects is the one
without principles or scruples. Moral authority
is the source of real leadership and is not
acquired easily but is based on a track record
of openness and fairness, respect for yourself
and respect for others.

Clarify your own goals and work on your own agenda

Develop a clear set of goals yourself and draft
your own agenda. The most effective politicians draft their manifestos with a clear set of
policy goals that they aspire to and will carry
out if given a mandate by the electorate.
People won't give you influence unless they
know what you propose to do with it. You
have to have that manifesto in place to gain
support – a clear view of your goals and how
those goals may be put into place. Sometimes,
you have to be flexible around the implemen-
tation of your goals but you should have a
clear idea of what you want to achieve before
you start to lobby and persuade.

If you don't have a clear agenda, then get
one. Go to the key stakeholders and understand their goals and identify how you can
help them achieve them. This is often a good
entry strategy within an organisation and

people you have helped are more likely to help you in return. You must have your own agenda – politicking and networking for their own sake is a very sterile occupation. Influencing people to accept an important agenda is a worthy and positive task and is politics in its most positive sense.

Having a clear set of goals that you can articulate clearly is an important feature in becoming influential. If others recognise that you have a clear personal agenda, then they will deal with you more effectively and your own level of influence will increase because you will be seen as someone who has something to add to the organisation. Without that clarity of goals, you will be likely to remain outside the circles of influence and those vitally important networks.

Learn to make deals and negotiate

Politicians can make deals and form coalitions and alliances with other politicians to achieve their policy goals. This doesn't mean that they have to agree wholly on every issue but that on a specific policy goal it is in their mutual interest to work together. This is an important factor in gaining influence within an organisation. Different people in different functions all have objectives that they want to achieve in order to be effective. Line managers want to see much higher results; functional specialists want to see the organisation become more professional within their area of expertise. Together, they can work on ways of developing new skills and capabilities which will lead to improved organisational performance.

Effective influencing and political operating

involves creating opportunities for mutual gain. In the real world of organisational politics there are times when it is necessary to become involved in issues in order to stop them happening and there are 'turf wars' where two people fight over a particular demarcation issue or compete for scarce resources. This is the negative side of politics and while you need to be alert to stopping these things happening, your focus must be on the identification of strategies and approaches that lead to mutual gain and a win–win solution for the protagonists and the organisation as a whole.

How good are your influencing and political skills?

Positive indicators for influencing and political skills

✎ Do you:

	YES	NO
have a positive network of contacts within your organisation that you can work with to achieve your personal or professional goals?	☐	☐
find it easy to gain the support of others for what you intend to do?	☐	☐
have goals that are aligned with those of your organisation? Are your proposals 'in flow' with the wider goals of the organisation?	☐	☐
understand how to make things happen within your business?	☐	☐

Negative indicators for influencing and political skills

✎ Do you:

	YES	NO
feel frustrated because your projects often die out through lack of support?	☐	☐
find yourself achieving other people's goals without any sense of achieving your own?	☐	☐
feel unsure of how to get things done within the organisation? Do you find that the levers of power are being pulled more effectively by other people?	☐	☐
feel that you don't have a clear personal agenda?	☐	☐

If the negatives outweigh the positives, then:

- clarify your own goals and objectives, setting them down clearly in writing
- list the people in the organisation who will (a) support and (b) block your goals
- try to imagine their comfort zones and write down what you see as their interests
- draw up a plan to make contact with them and confirm your initial analysis
- ensure you understand the strategy of the organisation and the key priorities. Is your work supporting those priorities?

....

BUILDING VISIBILITY

So far, most of the skills have assumed that you will be taking the initiative in approaching people in your network. The aim of good networking is to attract the right people to come to you. Networking becomes easier when you become the focus of other people's networking activities and when people start to say 'You should talk to xxxx, they have some interesting thoughts in that area', or 'You should call xxxx, they were really helpful to me over our change management project'. This requires building your visibility so that people know you and move towards you rather than you having to approach them.

The importance of building visibility

Building visibility is important because:

- you save time when people come to you and the discussions are on your terms
- people remember you – and in a world filled with subject experts to be memorable is an important differentiator
- you build your credibility and, more importantly, other people build it for you. Your reputation grows much faster when built by other people than it does when propelled by your own self-promotion.

Raising visibility

There are numerous strategies for raising visibility. I have clustered them into five groups:

- improving the quality of your work
- publicising your work
- teaching and developing others
- well-honed communication skills
- standing out from the crowd.

Improving the quality of your work

Visibility has to rest on a firm base. Developing visibility without improving performance is a dangerous strategy as it will produce the wrong sort of visibility – the spotlight that comes from doing a poor job. First, concentrate on increasing your contribution and creating a track record of high performance and achievement. Exceed your targets and deadlines; always keep your promises and exceed expectations and gain a reputation as someone who gets things done. Do this if you do nothing else in your visibility raising work.

Publicising your work

Let people know what sort of a job you are doing. Publicise your achievements and the successes of your team to a wider audience. Encourage visitors, write newsletters and make presentations about your work and the work of your section. Give your boss a note of your achievements before your performance appraisal so that they can be incorporated into your review notes. If you do good work in your organisation publicise it to your professional organisation and develop a reputation as an industry specialist. Don't claim more than you can accurately demonstrate, but don't keep your achievements and the achievements of your team hidden. Claim the credit but ensure that you share it with your colleagues or your team members. Developing a reputation as a 'credit hog' is the worst of all worlds for your reputation and your future networking plans.

Teaching and developing others

A reputation for developing and mentoring others is an important way to raise visibility. People don't just want to know what you have achieved but how you have achieved it. Everyone in business is searching for the secret of success and if you have a good track record everyone will want to find out how you have done it. Analyse your own skills and think through how you have done things, so that you can act as a mentor or coach to others. Participation in organisational training and development programmes will highlight your specialist expertise and a reputation as a skilled teacher will help you extend your network further afield.

Well-honed communication skills

Develop really excellent communication skills – both as a presenter and a writer. If you speak well and fluently, ensure that you find a good platform for your skills. Speak at meetings, dinners and training courses. If you are not a naturally good speaker, either go on a presentation skills course or develop a concise style and support your presentations with good and memorable handouts and visual aids.

Learn to be a concise writer – someone who

can summarise complex issues in a few concise pages or exhibits. Write brief articles for journals or newsletters, learn to write brief proposals for new ideas and write concise letters. Written communication is a permanent record of your thinking and you should see letters, reports and memos as an extension of your personal brand of communication.

Standing out from the crowd

Memorability is an important part of visibility. People who stand out from the crowd are more likely to remain visible and be approached by other people. People, like products, develop brands and become known for certain attributes. A brand is designed and developed to differentiate one product from another. Seeing yourself as a brand helps to differentiate you from other people with a similar background and experience. Standing out from the crowd helps to move you from someone in finance or 'a typical HR person' to 'Peter Jones who would be a really good person to get to speak to our divisional meeting about the re-engineering project' or 'Sally Robinson who has some interesting ideas about how we can improve our product development process'.

GOLDEN RULE 13

Become image conscious without becoming vain.

Brainstorm ways in which you can increase your memorability (without acting in a way that is out of character or will make you uncomfortable). Some thought starters are:

- Write a letter or article for a professional or in-house journal – it should be concise and focused but address an issue from a less conventional viewpoint.
- Learn to express yourself in an interesting way – speak in bold and colourful language.
- Remember people's names and use their name in conversation, and make sure that by the end of the discussion they remember your name.
- Ask questions at conferences and meetings – ask a short focused question and one which is approaching the issues from an interesting point of view.
- Read widely and expand your horizons from your current profession or industry to wider social and political issues.
- Express an interest in other people and follow up your discussions by sending them relevant articles from journals that they might not have read.

How good are you at building visibility?

Positive indicators for increasing visibility

✎ Do you:

	YES	NO
find that people contact you more than you contact them?	☐	☐

find that people seek you out at conferences or public events and introduce themselves? ☐ ☐

get asked to speak, write or chair meetings in your profession or organisation? ☐ ☐

get regular calls from headhunters? (Headhunters work through networks and the most visible people in an industry or profession will be known to them.) ☐ ☐

Negative indicators for increasing visibility

Do you:

	YES	NO
have to invest a lot of time in finding people to meet and talk to?	☐	☐
have to spend time at events trying to make new contacts?	☐	☐
feel isolated and undervalued within your organisation? Do other people with similar background and experience appear to progress further and faster than you do?	☐	☐

If you meet more negative criteria than positive, then you must work on this issue, otherwise your networking activity will be one-way traffic. When you make contacts, you need to ensure that they value your knowledge and personal qualities so much that they want to keep in touch and that they pass your name to other people so that your network grows and flourishes.

....

RECIPROCITY

GOLDEN RULE 14

Return favours.

Reciprocity deserves a brief section on its own. Reciprocity is an important element of networking in action and if there is a core principle to remember it is this – the networker variation of the old saying 'Do as you would be done by'.

Why is reciprocity important?

Reciprocity is important because:

- Networking is a two-way process. When either party ceases to gain benefit from the relationship, it ceases to function and loses its impetus.
- An active approach to reciprocity deepens the relationship faster as both parties appear to be gaining from it.
- Active focusing on reciprocity reduces the guilt of being seen to be using people, which is a barrier that prevents many people from networking.

How good are you at reciprocating?

Positive indicators for reciprocity

✎ Do you:

	YES	NO
think that your contacts gain as much from your relationship as you do?	☐	☐
find your networking meetings are easy to arrange and are a two-way conversation?	☐	☐
have some follow-up tasks to carry out from your meetings?	☐	☐

Negative indicators for reciprocity

✎ Do you:

	YES	NO
get the impression your meetings are an imposition on the other party?	☐	☐
feel guilty that you are imposing on the other person's time?	☐	☐
think there is little you can do to help your networking contacts?	☐	☐

If the negative responses outweigh the positive, you need to ensure that both parties gain from the networking experience. A simple approach is to develop some simple disciplines before, during and after networking meetings.

Before the meeting:

- Give as much time to thinking about the other person's goals and interests as you give to your own. See it as an important part of your preparation to anticipate their objectives.

- Carry out as much research as you can about the person you are meeting and their organisation. It will help you to understand them better and possibly suggest ways in which you can help them during the meeting. It also reduces the amount of time you spend in finding out facts which are already in the public domain, enabling you to concentrate on the really important issues that only your partner can explain.

During the meeting:

- Try hard to understand their viewpoint and explore their views with careful questioning. Check regularly to ensure that you are meeting their needs as well as your own.

- Clarify your own agenda at the beginning of the meeting and then ensure that you have given them an opportunity to clarify their agenda.

- Maintain a high degree of openness so that you are being as frank with them as they are with you. Give them some new information so that they feel that they are getting value from the time spent with you.

After the meeting:

- Follow up the meeting with a brief thank you note and make the note personal enough to say what you gained from the meeting. Carry out any agreed actions promptly.

- Keep their issues on your radar screen for the future and pass any relevant information on to them that you discover – this shows them that you have their interests at heart and keeps your needs at the front of their mind.

- Send articles, notes, cuttings and so on back to them as soon as possible after the meeting. These show that you have listened carefully to their interests and that you want to support them in achieving their objectives.

| GOLDEN RULE 15 |

Always follow up meetings.

Reciprocity is an important way of showing your network partners that you are as interested in their goals and aspirations as your own.

....

EXTENDING YOUR NETWORK

Networking is most definitely a lifelong activity. You need to build and develop your network over a period of time to meet your changing needs and to give you access to new ideas and contacts. Your network should not be a static thing and you shouldn't keep hold of the same people all the time. Networks bring you new ideas and keep your creativity fresh for the future and that is hard to do if you keep seeing the same old crowd.

The old boy network was such a deadly form of networking just because of this stasis. The same people with the same background and conditioning are highly unlikely to produce new and exciting ideas. They are more likely to recycle the old prejudices and resist new ideas.

Why is it important to extend your network?

It is important to extend your network because:

- your life changes and your needs change and so you need to meet new people with different experiences
- you need regular doses of new ideas and creativity that only new people can give you
- your value to network partners increases as your own network grows and develops.

How good are you at extending your network?

Positive indicators for extending your network

✎ Do you:

	YES	NO
frequently meet new people who stimulate you and introduce you to new ideas?	☐	☐
keep alert to opportunities to meet and get to know new people?	☐	☐
have a plan to extend your network?	☐	☐
include networking as part of your planning when you are going through changes in your life or work?	☐	☐

Negative indicators for extending your network

✎ Do you:

	YES	NO
spend time with the same group of people at meetings or social gatherings?	☐	☐
find it difficult to know who to contact when you have major changes in your life or work?	☐	☐

worry that your networking is
haphazard and unplanned?   ☐   ☐

If the negatives outweigh the positives, you
need to have a plan in hand to constantly
refresh your network and keep it fluid rather
than stagnant. There should be a flow in your
networking activity – some relationships naturally dry up while others grow and mature.
This is natural and perfectly sensible, otherwise we would still be going around with our
old school gang. Some ways to keep your
network fresh are:

- Meet more people – plan to get out of
  your office and meet new people. The
  more people you meet the better your
  chances of establishing good working
  relationships. Go to conferences,
  professional meetings and social events.
  Don't, however, take this advice to the
  extent that you don't do the other
  important things at work or that you
  break up your marriage by spending every
  night at some business dinner or other.

- Be alert for new opportunities when you
  meet people. Talk about your interests
  and ask them about theirs. Build rapport
  quickly and actively search for interests or
  activities in common. Don't go to an
  event and waste your time in idle
  conversation – learn to find out more
  about people quickly and be prepared to
  talk about yourself and your interests.
  Even at social events, become a good
  conversationalist – a good listener and an
  interesting talker – moving from trivia to
  more interesting topics early in the
  conversation.

- Exchange contact details. Make sure that you have a telephone number, address, fax number or e-mail address for the people with whom you want to keep in contact. If you feel embarrassed about this, develop a script or a comfortable form of words to use to enable you to do it easily and without awkwardness.

Keeping your network fresh will help you grow and develop. The people you meet are an important feature in your development. If you stay with the same old people then you will do the same old things and think the same old thoughts. New people, particularly those with experiences very different from yours, bring you new insights and perspectives which help you grow and mature.

GOLDEN RULE 16

Get out more.

....

KEEPING TRACK

Networking has some similarities to sheep herding. Your flock is spread out and one of your most important tasks is to keep track of individuals. You can't literally hire a sheep dog to nudge them into a pen together, but you can keep them together in the same place – your card file, Rolodex or contact manager. Keeping track takes a little time to set up but very little time to maintain if your system is working well.

Why is it important to keep track of your network?

You must keep track of your network because:

- people move around and you can't always assume that they will keep you up to date on their new address and contact numbers
- you need to have a systematic plan in place to keep in regular touch
- you build up a lot of knowledge about your contacts and you need to record the key facts about them, otherwise your knowledge is lost
- if you build up a good network you will have too many network contacts to enable you to rely on your memory alone.

GOLDEN RULE 17

Keep a good recording system for your network.

How good are you at keeping track?

Positive indicators for keeping track

✎ Do you:

	YES	NO
know how to contact your key contacts immediately?	☐	☐
have you a systematic plan for keeping in contact?	☐	☐
know and record some personal details about your contacts?	☐	☐

Negative indicators for keeping track

✎ Do you:

	YES	NO
find it difficult to keep hold of addresses and telephone numbers?	☐	☐
only contact people when you need to speak to them urgently?	☐	☐
know little about your contacts outside their work?	☐	☐

If the negatives outweigh the positives, begin to organise your contacts list so that you have a system for recording details of your contacts and of your meetings with them. There are several details that you need to keep.

Details on networker partners

Contact details

Ensure that you have your contacts' full addresses, telephone numbers (business, home and mobile), fax numbers, e-mail addresses and relevant Web site details.

Work interests

You should know the organisation they work for, their membership of professional institutes and the key interests that they have at the moment. You need to understand the current issues that are going on in their organisation in case you may be able to volunteer information when you see a relevant event in the press or on TV. There are few better ways of keeping a contact strong than by keeping in touch when you have something that is of interest to them. For example, if you know that a contact is in a business that is undergoing a reorganisation, and you send them a relevant article about re-engineering, you are sending them a number of messages:

1 You have their interests at the forefront of your mind and are keeping a look-out for them.

2 You are someone who has access to useful information.

3 You are a useful and helpful member of their network.

The principles of reciprocity work in this situation, as they will try to do something that will help you in the future.

Personal details

Remember earlier in the book we saw that 'people make friends before they make deals'? Knowing personal details about your network partners and their families puts your relationship beyond a purely transactional business contact towards a warm personal relationship. Details such as partner's and children's names and children's ages, family hobbies and sporting interests, home location, favourite holiday destinations are all things that you should know because they show a personal interest in your colleagues and indicate that you see the relationship as deeper than a transactional business contact.

A contact record

Keep a brief note of meetings and telephone contacts so that you can remember when you last met and the things that you agreed to do. Also, keeping a record helps you to develop a systematic approach to networking by keeping in more regular contact. Aim to make a certain number of networking calls each week, just to keep in touch or to pass on some small piece of relevant information. Find small personal reasons for making a call or a contact (a two-line e-mail takes seconds but puts you at the front of someone's mind and may lead to a renewed contact). Brainstorm some reasons for making a networking call to someone; here are a few starters:

- You read an article that their organisation is being taken over or is making an acquisition – call to see how this will affect your networking partner.
- Their favourite team wins an important

tournament – ring them to congratulate and celebrate.

- Their eldest daughter is taking her GCSEs – ring to ask how things are going.
- You have seen details of a conference or training programme that you think will interest them – send a copy with a covering note (add something like 'We must meet up in a few weeks, call me soon').

Recording all this information can be done either with paper and pencil or electronically. Pencil and paper is more difficult – index cards soon start to look dog-eared and become difficult to read. PC-based diary/contact manager programmes are easy to manage after the initial effort of recording addresses and numbers. If linked with a diary, you can also record and plan your contacts to link to a particular day or time of the year.

Networking is an important way to do business and develop yourself. You must work at it and one facet is to keep good records and to plan your networking activities. Make one call per day to maintain your network and aim to add one new person a week to your network. Do this over a period of years and you will grow a network that will be the envy of your friends … and, of course, by then you will certainly have a lot of friends.

RESILIENCE IN THE FACE OF FEAR AND OPPOSITION

Some people find networking easy; others find it more difficult. The people who find it more difficult often end up as better networkers than the naturals because they have to work at it and they learn some helpful techniques along the way. For most people, networking takes courage; sometimes you have to take some risks:

- making an initial contact with someone you want to meet
- meeting more senior and influential people
- asking favours from other people
- running the risk of being rejected by someone you have approached
- talking to strangers at conferences.

You will need to develop a greater resilience if you are to overcome your inhibitions and your fears about networking. This courage and self-confidence underpins all the preceding notes about skills and approach.

Why is resilience important?

Resilience is important because:

- you must feel confident when you approach someone – a half-hearted approach is worse than no approach at all
- you need to overcome your fear of 'using' people so that you feel you are entering into a relationship where both parties benefit
- networking should be one of the most enjoyable activities of your working life and so it should be fun. If it becomes a trial, you are not doing it right.

How resilient are you?

Positive indicators for resilience

✎ Do you:

	YES	NO
feel confident and positive when you approach people – particularly strangers or more senior people?	☐	☐
believe that they will gain as much from the discussion as you will?	☐	☐
find networking stimulating and exciting?	☐	☐

Negative indicators for resilience

✎ Do you:

	YES	NO
feel nervous and hesitant when you meet people?	☐	☐
feel that you are using them and taking up their time unreasonably?	☐	☐
find networking a trial and feel that you lose more than you gain?	☐	☐

If the negatives outweigh the positives, then:

- develop a 'script' or a set of introductory phrases for each meeting to help you into it more smoothly. As you get more

experienced the script will flow more naturally and you will work more effectively on autopilot
- focus on reciprocity – try to ensure that the other person gets at least the same value out of the relationship as you do, if not more. If the relationship is fully reciprocal then neither party need fear that they are using the other
- remember that networking is an important and perfectly valid part of organisational and commercial life. The most effective people are usually good networkers and have learned the power of having a good network in place
- relax and enjoy networking – it is an extension of making friends and we all enjoy doing that
- identify from this book which parts of networking you find the most difficult and then use the tips and techniques given to help you focus on that area. It isn't usually the whole concept of networking that people find difficult, it is normally one specific aspect that proves challenging
- develop some positive thinking about yourself, your value as a contact and your personal style. You must believe that you are a valuable person with a lot to offer and not a hanger-on or leech looking for contacts and back-handers.

GOLDEN RULE 18

Be bold in approaching people whom you want to meet.

....

SUMMARY

This part of *Powerful Networking* looked at the various skills the networker should develop and hone. You will have analysed how good you are at each of these skills and learnt ways of improving those that you are not quite so good at.

Remember, networking should be one of the most stimulating and enjoyable activities of your working life. If it isn't, you are doing it wrong and you need to stand back and analyse why.

The next part looks at networking in various situations.

Part four

NETWORKING IN SPECIFIC SITUATIONS

The previous sections have given you some general advice about networking skills and the type of people you need to have in place for your networking campaign. This section looks at some specific situations where you will find networking particularly useful and will identify some of the networking priorities that you will need to put into place in these scenarios. These are five of the most common situations and they are by no means exclusive:

- building business contacts when running your own business
- making a career change
- starting a new job
- developing your reputation as a professional
- returning to work or downshifting from full-time work.

....

BUILDING BUSINESS CONTACTS

Networking is a particularly important issue to the self-employed or small business owner. I have had two periods of self-employment and have known the importance of building a network of people as business contacts and for greater support. People prefer to do business with contacts that they know and trust. In certain service businesses – either consumer or business-to-business – a personal relationship is an important element in the choice of business adviser.

The really important decisions in our lives –

our choice of GP, our dentist, the school we send our children to, our solicitor and accountant – are usually based on personal recommendation. It is the same in business when people are choosing their PR adviser or a company to carry out some critical management training or the business who will do their contract cleaning. Networking helps to create those strong personal relationships which will not only get you some initial work but will be a source of the important recommendations that you need for future business.

Creating good quality connections

The following paragraphs give some tips on creating a flow of good quality connections.

Start networking early, even before you make the move into your own business. Remember that people make friends before they make deals and this takes time and patience. There is usually a long period between making a contact and turning that contact into a productive business relationship – understanding their needs, their developing faith in your ability to deliver, finding a good opportunity to work together and agreeing a pilot activity – these phases all take time and cannot be rushed, particularly as you can't always set the pace for activities that take place inside the client's business.

Look for new ideas and not just contacts. Working in a small business usually gives you access to fewer ideas than you might find working in a larger business. You have to go out and find new ideas and new approaches to your work, otherwise you find yourself quickly selling yesterday's solutions to today's problems. Your network should include catalysts and provocateurs to stimulate your thinking and keep your ideas bank in credit.

Remember your professional and personal development. If you are running a small business, you won't have the same access to training and development specialists to support your personal development. It is unlikely that you will have the budget or the time to go on lengthy training programmes and so you must find coaches and mentors to help you grow and develop both professionally and personally.

Running your own business can be a lonely and stressful occupation. You may have pulled out of the rat race but you have to continually manage to deliver this week's business while finding next week's new business. Networking with other small businesses can help to reduce the solitude by talking about your problems. It can also lead to collaboration with other businesses to produce a new and exciting product or service.

As a small business, you are your own PR and advertising department – you can't afford to take out a full page advert in *The Times* and so you have to be prepared to sell your services and to make as many contacts as you can. Many of us find it easier to talk to people we know than to make cold calls – most of your work, at least initially, will come from your core contacts. How your business grows will be a factor of how you extend this network and how you increase the numbers of people who believe you are the right person to help them with their business problems.

....

MAKING A CAREER CHANGE

Changing your career or your job is one of the most exciting or the most difficult times in your working life. Years ago working lives were spent in the same business or profession, making the occasional incremental change by promotion to the next grade and occasionally moving to a new business. Now, most people make three or four major job moves within their career – either moving to a new organisation or making significant moves within their current business.

Networking is an important part of making a career change, not just to make contacts but also to research new options and to keep in touch with the current labour market. People who are made redundant after twenty-five or thirty years in one organisation are only at a disadvantage if they have no idea of the external market for their industry or profession. In the volatile business climate that we are working in today, and in the future, to have no idea of the outside market smacks of almost criminal negligence, leaving people with no real understanding of new job opportunities, the new skills they need to develop and the people who can help them.

Networking for career change

Effective networking for career change involves an iteration between clarifying your career goals and finding out more about new opportunities which can create new ideas as you refine your career goals.

Make your plans for career change well in advance of actually making the change. Many people fail to take any action to make a change until it is too late to do so. Change is best planned when things are going well, while there is still plenty of scope to grow and develop in your current situation. Most people, however, only make changes when they are forced upon them and then have to make hurried adjustments to their career plan, moving swiftly and surely from the frying pan into the fire. If you are enjoying your work and getting a sense of satisfaction from it, then now is the time to start thinking about your next career move while you feel relaxed and confident.

Clarify your career goals now without being too rigid. Before you start networking to support a career change, try to clarify broadly where you are now in terms of skills and motivation and then consider where you want to be in both the long and medium term. You don't need to be too rigid – your networking meetings will help to clarify your career objectives and may introduce you to new ideas and opportunities that lead to more interesting ways of achieving your goals.

Use your network to help you survey the available opportunities and not just to help you find a new job. If you leave your networking 'campaign' to the last minute, then you will find yourself desperately hoping that your network partners will help you find a job. This air of desperation is rarely helpful as it raises the stakes for each of your networking meetings and leads to frustration which may damage your working relationships.

In your survey meetings, be prepared to articulate your broad goals but don't make the agenda too specific. You are looking for new ideas and opportunities rather than developing a detailed career plan. Identify the sort of organisation you want to work for and try to find someone in that organisation or someone who can help you find someone who works there. Approach them with a view to finding out more about their business and more about what they do and the important things you need to know about them – people find this approach much more acceptable than an obvious appeal for a job.

Do your homework beforehand. Much of the information you seek is in the public domain and busy people find it tiresome to explain things that are already available. You should use the precious face-to-face networking time to gain the sort of information that isn't in books or periodicals – the really important information that is locked inside people's heads. If you were going to climb Everest you wouldn't ask 'Where is it?' or 'How high is it?' – but you might ask about the right ways to prepare for the climb or the techniques that proved the most effective for crossing an ice wall.

GOLDEN RULE 19

Do research before meeting new networkers.

....

STARTING A NEW JOB

One of the most neglected factors in job induction is developing a powerful network of people both inside and outside the organisation. Your first task in a new job, apart from finding the toilets and the canteen, is to put in place a network of people who can help you understand the business and support you in setting and achieving your working goals. You must develop good working relationships with your boss, direct reports and your immediate colleagues – this much is obvious. However, you must also develop good working relationships with others in the organisation and outside. Some useful members of this network would be:

- colleagues who have a clear grasp of the organisation's future – these are the people who can give you clues about the future agenda for the organisation and the likely priorities for your own role
- the formal network in your organisation – the people with authority who, although they may not help you achieve your objectives, can prevent you from achieving them
- your key stakeholders – the people who are your key customers or suppliers in the organisation or externally. Managing your own supply chain is an important early win in your new job as both parties can either enhance your reputation at an early stage or damage it. Coming into a new job, you are able to discard most of the baggage of your predecessor and can make a good early start with your stakeholders

by understanding their objectives, the problems they face and the help that you can offer them

- the informal network of people who are trusted and who have influence on the way things are done in the organisation. These are the 'gatekeepers' to the important networks in the organisation and are people you need to influence if you are to have any real influence

- external advisers to the organisation – these are people who can help you see the organisation from a different perspective. Although they will be influenced by their own interests and their desire to remain an adviser to the business, they be the source of useful information and a more detached perspective of the politics or the organisation and the networks that they find useful in order to gain influence.

Get to see these people at an early stage in your induction and ensure that you have a clear script when you meet them. They must get a sense of your agenda early in the discussions and the value that you can add to their work. Reciprocity is important here and you should ensure that the relationship isn't just a one-way street.

Remember, you are building a long-term relationship that may extend beyond the boundaries of your current role in the organisation, and so you must behave in a way that positions you as a professional and competent addition to the organisation and someone who can help get things done. The networks you make at an early stage in your new role can be critical in your success in your current organisation, and these contacts may form the basis for networks during the rest of your working life.

....

DEVELOPING YOUR REPUTATION AS A PROFESSIONAL

This is one of the skills of networking we have already touched on. It is important to grow your reputation as either an industry expert or a professional. This is a networking activity that should carry on in parallel with any other activities that you are working on. It is too easy to dismiss professional networking as a 'nice to do' rather than a 'must do'. The colleagues within your organisation may not see the point of this part of your networking campaign, but it is important that you maintain contacts in the wider network so that you have a network in place to help you when you need it.

Keeping your networks in place

Networking is an activity that should be carried out when you least need it. It should be an important rather than an urgent activity. If you find yourself networking in crisis, then you have been neglecting your networks for too long.

In order to keep your wider networks in place, make a point of joining two or three professional or industry institutes – perhaps one related to your profession and one to your industry. You may also consider joining a wider business organisation such as the Institute of Directors or your local Chamber of Commerce. Your choice of organisation depends largely on your long-term career goals. If you see yourself as a human resources specialist you will focus more on the Institute of Personnel Development or the Association for Management Education and Development; if you see yourself as a retail industry specialist, you will focus more on the Institute of Grocery Distribution.

Joining an organisation should normally give you access to a newsletter or journal and this will help your professional development and keep you up to date with the key changes in the profession or industry. This is still a very passive approach to networking and if you want to gain more from your relationship you need to attend meetings and contribute more actively to the work of the institute. You may have to make a decision to focus on one organisation as it is too easy to over-commit to meetings and conferences at the expense of your other development activities.

Use your membership as a platform for your work by offering to speak at conferences or, if you feel you don't have enough presentation material yet, to chair meetings or lead discussions. As well as raising your profile, you will learn some valuable skills in leading and facilitating meetings.

Attend at least one conference or training programme each year – your professional updating is particularly important and you can combine the event with some serious contact making. Choose your conference with care and view it from the perspective of both your current priorities and your future aspirations.

GOLDEN RULE 20

Network more when you don't need to.

....

RETURNING TO WORK OR DOWNSHIFTING FROM FULL-TIME WORK

The networking scenarios described above are activities that require moving from one work-based situation to another. Another situation where networking is important is making the move back to work after a long break. For many women, the most common reason for this is the return to work after a career break or maternity leave. The same issues can be faced by people retiring from a large organisation such as the police or the armed services, making a move into a completely different commercial environment.

Both groups are approaching a world where they may feel they have fewer contacts and little understanding of the way things are done. They need the security of a good network to help them develop new skills and make new contacts in order to begin what is effectively a new career. There are two important factors to think through before beginning such a campaign:

- What are your career goals – what sort of a role are you looking for and how do you see yourself balancing this role with other facets of your life?

- What current networks do you belong to and what sorts of contacts do you have presently?

As already pointed out, suddenly trying to acquire a network is a difficult thing to achieve. You need to be developing and maintaining a network for some time before you can call on it in an emergency. The good news is that you probably have a very significant network in place but may not have seen it as such until reading this book. Think of your social networks, your friends, your membership of various societies, your hobbies and recreations – all of these will come with a ready-made network.

If you have a clear idea of what you want to achieve in your return to work or your move out of a long-term career, then you should start to discuss these ideas with other people in your network as soon as possible. At the beginning, your need is for information and, perhaps, a little education about the world that you are moving into. You can start by 'surveying' the scene and trying to find people who will give you useful advice and possibly make other contacts for you. Friends and their spouses, other family contacts, fellow school governors and members of your sports clubs can all be good sources of further contacts or ideas and advice. You need to do the following:

- Think about your future career goals and identify the sorts of things you would like to work on in the future. Even if it is two or three years away, you can't start networking early enough as you are building up a contact base for the rest of your life and you need to allow a period for growing and developing a more enduring relationship.

- Learn to talk to people about your aspirations and the things that you want to do. Don't feel self-conscious about talking about yourself as many people are only too interested in other people's plans. People with aspirations and ideas are much more interesting to talk to than people who are content to let life drift by. If you start to talk about your plans you may stimulate other people to think about their lives and you may become a catalyst for some exciting projects.

- Ask people about their ideas and their aspirations. Show the same interest in their goals as you would expect them to show in yours.

....

SUMMARY

In this section I have outlined five common scenarios that people face in establishing and maintaining their network. You should now have a good idea as to how to approach these situations. The final section of the book summarises the twenty golden rules for powerful networking with some action points to get you started.

Part five

TAKE ACTION – USING THE TWENTY GOLDEN RULES FOR POWERFUL NETWORKING

Networking is one of the approaches to the new world of work that you should find the most enjoyable. Once you have made a start, you will find that many of your work-based problems will be resolved. You will start to generate new ideas and will find a good contact to help you with most of your problems. The most important thing is to start to do it now – these twenty golden rules will help you to develop an action plan. Each rule is accompanied by some action points to help you prioritise your networking campaign.

....

THE GOLDEN RULES

Rule 1.
Use networking as an important part of your personal development

Look for mentors, coaches and role models to help your development – these people can make a real difference to your future by giving you feedback and giving you access to new ideas and different ways of looking at the world.

Actions

- Identify mentors and coaches on your list. A good coach or mentor is a tremendous development mechanism. Research done several years ago for company directors put 'working for a good boss' up with 'gaining early managerial responsibility' as a key factor in their development.

- Make the relationship more formal. Ask people to act as your coach or your mentor and make a contract with them about the way you feel you can benefit from their support. Don't let the relationship drift into aimless socialising but firm the relationship up into a more purposeful and productive element of your development.

Rule 2.

Map out your current network

You already know many people with whom you can exchange support, ideas and contacts. Before going off on a networking campaign, sit down and map out your existing list of contacts.

Actions

- Write down a list of the possible networks to which you already belong. Write down the organisations you have worked for, your membership of professional institutes, hobbies and recreations, membership of social groups, committees you sit on, family members, educational establishments and social contacts.

- List the people you know within these groupings. Note down all the names you remember in each of the groupings, underline those where you have had some quite recent contact. They are the most

likely priorities for the first phase of your
networking campaign.

- Note down any other possible linkages
between your network and other
networks. Make a note of any of your
contacts that you know have connections
to other networks or organisations. They
may well be good gatekeepers who can
give you access to other people within
their own network.

Rule 3.
**Develop a broad network of people who
can support you in different ways**

Networking is not just about getting a job or
finding new business. Your network needs to
be full of people with whom you have different relationships and who add something
different to your own approach to life.

Actions

- Take your list of contacts and identify
where they are most likely to add value.
Take the list of networking types –
mentors, soul mates, coaches and so on
and note down where your current
contacts fit against this list. Identify the
categories where you have a relatively
large number of contacts and those where
you have a smaller number. Think
laterally about how you might fill any
gaps and think through what it may say
about your approach to networking – do
you have lots of soul mates but no

mentors? Or several authority figures but
no provocateurs?

- Look for a broad network. When you start
  to network, try to target people who you
  feel could fill the gaps in your network
  group. If you need a mentor, then try to
  identify people who you feel would make
  good and supportive mentors; if you feel
  your network is a little too comfortable,
  go out and find people who you think
  will provoke and stimulate you.

Rule 4.

Avoid networking with people who drain you of energy

Where possible, create a network of people
who support your goals. Avoid people who are
cynical about your goals or who you find
difficult to relate to. You should enjoy networking and gain something positive from it;
it shouldn't be a stressful or difficult exercise.

Action

- Identify the cynics and stress carriers in
  your network. List the people who you
  find difficult or scratchy. Then ask
  yourself if there is a wider benefit that
  you gain from working with them. If they
  add value in some other way, perhaps you
  shouldn't write them off. You may have a
  mentor who you find particularly challenging – ask yourself if that challenge
  acts as a stimulus for you to do better or
  is it just a painful process. If it is the former,

then you should find ways to deal with the challenge; if the latter, then allow the relationship to wither on the vine.

Rule 5.

Understand your own personal networking style

Never act out of character or try to do something in a way that isn't natural to you. Some people find networking very easy and are able to be bold in approaching others; some less venturesome people find it difficult and need to find an approach that suits them.

Actions

- Work on the questionnaire in part Two. Fill in the questionnaire – it may give you some ideas about your own style and your motivation to start networking.

- Get feedback from other people. Ask people who know you well about your style and approach to networking. Your spouse or a good friend may be a good source of feedback. Look for someone who will give you feedback while protecting your self-esteem! You don't want so much feedback that you can't leave the house for a week. Ask some specific questions about how you add value to other people and then ask for ideas about developing your networking style – are you too intrusive or too reticent in your approach to others? Are you supporting other people or do you focus exclusively on your own objectives?

- Take opportunities for formal assessment. If your organisation runs assessment techniques such as 360° feedback, development centres or career reviews, then volunteer for them or try to identify how you can participate. Understanding your personal style and having feedback from a trained practitioner is a tremendously useful, if occasionally disconcerting, experience. It will help you understand the implications of your personal style.

Rule 6.

Find ways to make connections with people for your networks quickly

The first part of building good networking relationships is to develop ways to make contact with people quickly. Examine your life and try to identify new opportunities for making stronger connections with people.

Actions

- Take your network list and identify ways to make faster connections. How might you make a connection with some of the people on your contact list? Brainstorm things that you have in common with the people in your networking list and try to think of possible connections with others who seem to be less obvious.

- Focus on making connections. At any event that you attend think about the possible connections that you can make with others. Make a game of thinking how quickly you can make links with other people and how you can make the fastest connections into each situation. Without making connections, all other networking activities are useless and it is important to develop 'connecting skills', particularly if you are more introverted and find the initial introduction difficult.

Rule 7.

Use different media to keep in touch with your network

There are many more ways to keep in touch with people today than there ever were. Mobile telephones, e-mail, video conferencing and the fax machine have all added to our capacity for flexible communication. Keeping in touch can be done more quickly now than ever before and you should use this range of approaches to maintain your network. A one-line e-mail takes seconds to write but is an effective way to keep in contact.

Actions

- Ensure that you are contactable at all sensible times. Ensure that you have the media you need to be easy to contact – telephone, mobile telephone, fax, answerphone and e-mail address would seem to be the basic accoutrements for a networking campaign. Ensure that all relevant numbers and addresses are on your business card and letter heading and that you can be contacted when you are away from your office – through a mobile phone, answerphone or a secretary/PA.

- Get yourself on e-mail. E-mail is a great networking medium – instant, quick and paper-free with direct access to your contact and no waiting to connect calls. Get yourself on e-mail as quickly as you can and your networking capacity will grow tremendously.

Rule 8.

Try to get on people's wavelengths as quickly as possible

An important skill in networking is to build rapport with people quickly so that you can both move from superficial to meaningful conversation as quickly as possible. You will do this by tuning in to their wavelength and developing a good relationship based on their comfort zones, not by expecting people to tune in to your wavelength.

Actions

- Learn 'rapport building' skills. Observe good sales people ('good' meaning people who make you want to buy and not people who have a sales routine) and see how they build rapport with their clients or customers. Keep your antennae out for good service providers and see how they quickly adopt the right approach to suit the situation and the client.

- Observe your contacts closely. Make a point of observing your contacts to understand their interest and to see how they approach issues. Observe actively, noting the issues that they feel strongly about and the way that they approach them. Initially you should work hard to get on their wavelength in order to move the relationship forwards more quickly.

Rule 9.
Be open about your own goals and aspirations

Once you have developed a relationship of trust it is important to let people know your own agenda to enable them to contribute or give you support – often in ways that you may not have considered.

Action

- Clarify your goals and aspirations. Before you can share them, you will need to clarify them. Many people network aimlessly without any sense of purpose. You need to do some work to think about:
  - your career goals – the industry or profession where you see yourself working
  - your objectives for your current job (aim for the three or four things that you really want to achieve)
  - your capabilities and those areas where you could use some more support.

Rule 10.
Understand other people's goals and interests before focusing on your own

Stephen Covey in *The Seven Habits of Highly Effective People* encourages people to 'seek first to understand ... then to be understood'. Effective networking is based on empathetic communication and not an insensitive pushing of your own agenda at the expense of other people's.

Actions

- Before every meeting, spend time planning the other person's agenda. You should be spending as much time thinking about the other person's agenda as you do your own. After each meeting, try to write down a brief synopsis of the other person's position so that you have that as clearly in your mind as your own idea and interests.

- Understand the needs of your network. Take some of the people that you know well on your networking list and note down the most critical issues in their working lives and how you can add value to them.

Rule 11.
Build long-term relationships based on mutual understanding

Networking is a lifelong process and our objective should be to make long-term, enduring relationships which will provide mutual support for many years and not quick transactions to extract maximum advantage from a contact before moving on to someone else. Good relationships are built on trust and a sense of mutual advantage; these develop and endure over time and become an even greater benefit to both parties.

Actions

- Analyse your closest relationships and try to identify what makes them effective. Are there particular themes that recur and which may be useful clues to making your other relationships more effective and productive?

- Identify the relationships you want to develop. Look at the relationships you most want to develop more closely (perhaps with a good 'gatekeeper' or a potential mentor) and make a plan to make them more productive and enduring. What approaches will turn a simple working relationship into a deeper and more trusting personal relationship? Different things will work for different people and you should examine your relationships one by one to better understand what will work for different members of your network.

Rule 12.
Become an interesting conversationalist

Good relationships are based on more than a set of shared interests. You should also enjoy a person's company and be stimulated by the time you spend with them. Likewise, the relationship will only work if they feel the same about you. You must learn to be a good conversationalist – that means being both a good talker and a good listener.

Actions

- Broaden your interests. Learn to talk about things other than banking or human resource management or whatever is your main professional interest. Broaden your interests both at work and in your social life. Sometimes we focus so much on our narrow goals that we forget how many interesting ideas and contacts we can make when we relax and start to think about other things. We have to learn when to be focused, concentrating on our goals and objectives, and when to be more free thinking, allowing ourselves to think outside our narrow framework.

- Practise active listening. Find out as much as you can about the people you are dealing with by asking them open questions and focusing on their needs rather than your own. Asking interesting questions about their background and experience – questions that may make them think differently about themselves – will make you appear to be a valuable member of their network because you are interested in their problems and issues as well as your own.

Rule 13.

Become image conscious without becoming vain

The image you present to the world is a very important factor in the development of your network. It can be either an asset or a liability.

Actions

- Ask a good friend for feedback. Ask for feedback on the impression you make on others. Accept the feedback positively and without defensiveness and work to develop your positive points and mitigate your negative points. People are like products – they have a brand image and you need to make sure that your brand image is the one that you want to project to enable you to achieve your goals.

- Create a professional image with your communication. Look carefully at your written communication. What does it say about you? Well-typed letters on good quality writing paper say that you are professional and businesslike. Badly produced written work says that you are not really taking your communication seriously or that your standards of presentation are low. Design your stationery, business cards and the typeface you use in order to ensure that your image in writing projects the same messages that you would want to project face to face.

Rule 14.
Return favours

Don't create a one-way street in your relationships. If someone does you a favour or provides you with help or support, try to identify ways in which you can reciprocate. Reciprocity is an important factor in effective networking. If both parties benefit, the relationship grows and develops; your contact is likely to introduce you to others because of your ability to add value to a relationship.

Action

- Think reciprocity before and after
  meetings. Before each meeting, try to
  understand what you can do for your
  contact and, likewise, after the meeting
  think through if there are any things that
  you can do that will make a helpful
  follow-up for your network partner.

Rule 15.

Always follow up meetings

Your mother probably taught you to write
thank you notes for parties. In the skills of
networking, this moves beyond politeness to
effectiveness. Always drop people a note or
call them to thank them for their time in
seeing you – this is simple courtesy. When you
write to them just highlight a couple of the
important points that you want them to do or
remember from your discussion – a concise
follow-up helps to ensure that your agenda
stays with them some time after the meeting
has finished.

Actions

- Build the follow-up into your network
  discipline. Immediately after every meeting get into the habit of noting down
  any action points and the key issues
  you discussed. Use those as the basis
  for your follow-up note after the meeting.

- After a meeting, think about the messages
  that you want to leave behind and to
  reinforce. These should be reflected in
  your follow-up note.

Rule 16.

Get out more

The key to effective networking is to start it by just going around more to different events – to conferences, professional meetings, societies – the more people you meet the greater your chance of developing a large network. You can always refine and develop more effective plans for networking but as Lao Tse said, 'The journey of a thousand miles starts with a single step' … outside your office door.

Actions

- Look for opportunities to network. Look for meetings to attend, people to talk to and get out of your office and start networking with the people around you. Don't eat your lunch in your own office every day. Go to the staff restaurant where you just might meet someone to talk to about work, the news, or anything that might lead to an interesting discussion.

- Check your diary. Look back over the last six months and check how many meetings and external visits you have made. Set yourself a target to beat that in the next six months.

Interesting stuff doesn't just come into your office – you have to go out and find it.

Rule 17.

Keep a good recording system for your network

Keep track of people in your network and the important contact numbers. Also ensure that they know how to contact you, particularly if you move jobs. Tom Peters in his book *The Pursuit of Wow* notes: 'Your power is almost directly proportional to the thickness of your Rolodex and the time you spend maintaining it'. Keep a record of your network partners – particularly the key facts about them and the things that are important to them.

Actions

- Get a recording system set up immediately. You must have a good recording system in place before you start your networking campaign. You need to record the meetings you have had and you must have contact details of your network readily available, preferably in one place. Whether you choose a relatively simple system based on card index files or a PC-based system, you must keep some records and be in a position to update them. Your contact list should be one of the first things you rescue from a fire!

- Keep notes. Keep brief notes of your networking meetings for future reference. Networking shouldn't be a huge bureaucratic burden but it is an important business process which should be managed. Notes and records make it more systematic and professional – an extension of the persona you aim to show your networking partners.

Rule 18.

Be bold in approaching people whom you want to meet

Good business relationships are based on empathy and impact. Good sales people have both the empathy to understand the needs of their customers and the boldness to approach people and achieve their own personal objectives. Learn to overcome your fear of rejection and approach people who you feel could help you in your career or your business.

Actions

- Develop a script. Write down a set of scripts for some of the people you might want to meet. Write the script in long-hand and refer to it often, but obviously don't read from it when you meet people! The most difficult part of meeting people is the introduction and if you can develop a good introductory script then you will enter discussions with more confidence and the remainder of the discussion will flow more naturally. People want to know what you want from them quickly and once that is clear they relax and open up. Include in your opening script a clear idea of who you are, your aspirations and why you are approaching them. Do this for some of the people you want to include in your network.

- Overcome your fear of rejection. Don't feel concerned if some people don't respond well to your initial overtures. They may have their own reasons for not wanting a meeting and the likelihood is that this is nothing to do with you but may be due to some other things that are going on in their lives – they may be too busy or preoccupied with other things at the time. You shouldn't feel that because one person has not followed up your suggestion no one else will. The other part of the sales personality – the ego drive – is important here. You need to stand back and think about your own aspirations and gain strength from your desire to achieve them. Keep going forward and meeting new people. The world is full of people who are willing and able to help you achieve your goals. See any rejection as a sign that a particular relationship is not for you – don't take it personally.

Rule 19.
Do research before meeting new networkers

When you do approach people show respect for their time by not asking them things you could have found out more easily in other ways. You don't want to waste time in a brief meeting with a busy senior executive by asking questions that are easily answered by your own desk research elsewhere. Use the time to discuss issues of value, not exchanging facts which could easily be discovered elsewhere.

Actions

- Gather a 'virtual' library. You need to know where you can find things quickly about a business or an idea without gathering together a great pile of documents and books. Sources such as the World Wide Web have given access to so much information that we can use without gathering together a mass of books and papers. Get yourself on the Internet and try to find information on a target business or organisation. Many organisations have a Web site which enables you to find out some of the basic information about products, services, ethos and structure without having to spend valuable networking time on issues that are already in the public domain. You will also find that major institutes have libraries and research facilities that can help you do your basic research before your meetings. Build yourself a virtual library of information contacts so that you know where to do your research when you need to do it.

- Be better read. There are increasing expectations that people in business or in oganisational life generally will be better informed than in the past. You should know something about a wide range of business and management techniques, so that you don't have to spend valuable face-to-face networking time finding out things that you can learn through book tapes in your car or through reading on the train. There will be some issues that you need to understand better than others – these will probably be connected to your profession or industry – but you need to maintain your broader business literacy by reading journals such as the *Economist* or the *Harvard Business Review* as well as journals about your profession or business sector.

Rule 20.

Network more when you don't need to

Networking involves initiating and developing long-term relationships based on mutual trust and respect. It is not a good policy to contact people only when you need their help. If you only call when you have been made redundant or when you want contacts to help you with a business proposition, your network will soon dry up. Network more actively when things are going well so that you build up the quality of relationship which can provide support when you need more active help.

Actions

- Start your campaign now. Networking is a lifelong activity and you should start your campaign now so that you lose no tme in building these really important relationships. Whoever you start with, at least start somewhere and with someone in order to get into the disciplines and approaches of good networking.

- Start with the low hanging fruit. Approach people with whom you feel confident and relaxed. Don't head straight for the chairman of Shell or the Home Secretary until you feel more confident in your style and approach. If you see networking as a lifelong task, take one step at a time and build up your contacts systematically. People who neglect their networking partners and then rush at them when they lose their jobs or they need new business contacts put themselves under more pressure because they are trying to force the pace. Good working relationships have to grow and mature slowly – they can't be manufactured quickly. So start now.

....

SUMMARY

Networking is becoming a key part of getting on in today's business. *Powerful Networking* has shown you what networking means, the benefits of it and how you can make positive steps towards doing it. The twenty rules expanded on in the text and summarised in this chapter will help you with effective networking.

REFERENCES
AND FURTHER
READING

Clutterbuck, David, *Everyone Needs a Mentor*, IPD, 1978

Covey, Stephen, *The Seven Habits of Highly Effective People*, Simon & Schuster, 1992

De Geus, Arie, *The Living Company*, Nicholas Brealey, 1997

Goleman, Daniel, *Emotional Intelligence*, Bloomsbury, 1996

Kelley, Robert, and Caplan, Janet, 'How Bell Labs Create Star Performers', *Harvard Business Review*, July/Aug 1993

Kelley, Robert, *Star Performer*, Orion Business, 1998

McDermott, Ian, and Shircore, Ian, *NLP and the New Manager*, Orion Business, 1998

Moss Kanter, Rosabeth, *World Class*, Simon & Schuster, 1997

Peters, Tom, *The Pursuit of Wow*, Macmillan, 1995

INDEX